# History Galore

## GHOST TOWNS
## AND MORE

# Carol George Bernhardt

## EDITED BY ANN NORRIS BAILLY

History Galore
Ghost Towns and More
All Rights Reserved.
Copyright © 2013 Carol George Bernhardt
Edited by Ann Norris Bailly
v2.0

Outskirts Press, Inc.
http://www.outskirtspress.com

ISBN: 978-1-4787-0877-3

Outskirts Press and the "OP" logo are trademarks belonging to
Outskirts Press, Inc.

PRINTED IN THE UNITED STATES OF AMERICA

outskirtspress
DENVER, COLORADO

# Contents

Introduction................................................................. i

Dedication ................................................................ iii

Section 1
    Anaconda to Wickes................................................ 1

Section 2
    Aldridge to Storrs.................................................. 51

Section 3
    Ingomar to Ismay ................................................ 73

Section 4
    Burke to Saltese .................................................. 76

Section 5
    Havre to Zortman ................................................ 90

Section 6
    Enchanted Highway to Medora Musical............................... 99

Forts of the 1800s ...................................................... 103

# Introduction

THIS BOOK IS a compilation of twelve years of my husband Dave Bernhardt and me reading dozens of books on western history and especially focusing on old mining and ghost towns. We were fascinated with the stories and decided that we wanted to see these places first hand. My mother Hallie George Praye started the whole thing: she gave Dave a book for Father's Day in about 1995. It was Don Miller's book Ghost Towns of Montana. The places Miller photographed and told about in his book were our first chosen "explorations." Long before we retired, we set out on weekends to locations close to Billings such as Kendall and Giltedge near Lewistown and Bearcreek out of Red Lodge. Eventually, it became a driving force in our lives:—find another mine or ghost town in one of our books, locate the area on the Montana map, and set aside time to get there. Many places were far off the beaten path. By far the majority of mining towns were in the more mountainous areas of western Montana. Sometimes we took our car instead of our pickup and lived to regret it. Some road surfaces were terribly rocky or deeply rutted. Twice I remember walking ahead of the car picking up big rocks off the road and throwing them out of the roadway ahead of us! When it happened in the hills south of Butte, a couple on a motorcycle drove by laughing and then advised us to give up. They knew the road surface wasn't going to improve. We turned around. For a couple years, we traveled in a little motorhome, but it was too low to the ground or too tall for some tree branches.

Everything is true in this book. I tried really hard to be accurate on how to locate ghost towns or mines if readers want to visit them. Many chapters were written from the journaling I did as we traveled. When we returned home, Dave and I worked together to make sure that we had identified our photos correctly and then I made a file for each site we had found.

Dave had a gift of making friends with strangers immediately. We both knew that some of the best stories about history could be found in local people. We usually looked for some gray-haired individual. So many times we had to depend on asking questions to get the correct road and directions to a mining area because signs were sorely lacking. Occasionally, we would see an upright post that we were sure had supported a road sign. State maps don't have adequate space for each little town of only 40 people.

Now you probably won't believe this, but we have some really great photos of most of these historic places and all we ever had for a camera was a 35mm with rolled film! Everyone told us that we needed to buy a digital, but it just never happened.

Until the day that I die and join Dave, I will forever treasure the memories of all these trips across Montana and nearby states and all the wonderful people that we met. I need to thank the people that we met on our travels and also the many friends that have encouraged me in this endeavor to write a book to honor my dear husband and to help others explore some of the "backroads of the West. I hope you will enjoy reading this book as much as I enjoyed recording our adventures.

# Dedication

THIS BOOK IS dedicated to my dear husband David Lee Bernhardt who was raised in Laurel, Montana. At age 69 in April of 2011 he died of a heart attack. His cardiologist had planned to schedule open heart surgery. We were married over 42 years. Dave was one of a kind—a man of principles and a devoted husband, father, and grandfather.

He was the driving force behind all our travels of Montana and nearby states to search out old mining towns, old forts, and historic sites. It became contagious and I was just as enthusiastic as him after our first couple trips leaving Billings. Dave made the preparations for our adventures—putting gas in our car or pickup, selecting the best regional maps, loading our vehicle, etc. His 39 years of experience with the Montana Highway Dept. gave him good travel skills and knowledge of many roads. His sense of direction was amazing. I never could have found these out-of-the-way places, let alone kept from getting lost. He always knew how to navigate us back to an Interstate or primary road.

Dave loved to share our latest excursions or historic facts with family, friends, or people who worked at businesses we often frequented. Those are the people who asked how this book was coming. One lady's remark was that she never did like history in school, but Dave gave her a new perspective on it and she would like to find some of these places we located.

I am very thankful that we got to have these adventures and that

Dave put a priority on our time together rather than on a hobby or a new car. We shared such joy when we found beautiful scenery miles from civilization (not quite!) or came upon intact buildings or mine equipment in a ghost town. We tried to visit museums when it was feasible, also.

# Anaconda to Wickes

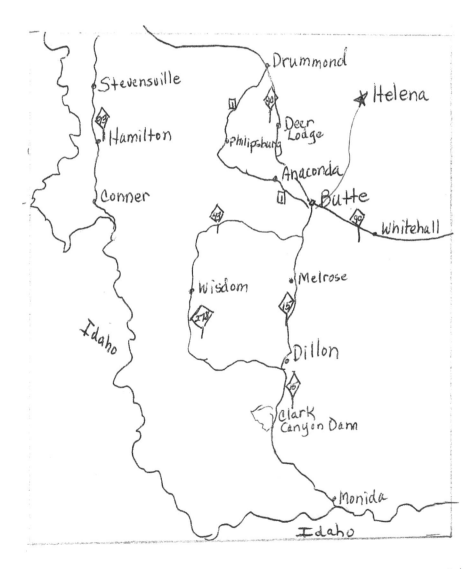

**ALHAMBRA, MT,** lies about 15 miles south of Helena on Highway 212. A prominent hot springs spa enterprise can easily be seen from the road. It appears to be promoted as a health resort now. Since our goal was to find the history of the old mining camp, Dave drove down the road past the spa to investigate the area. We both looked along the road for any signs of the town's historic past. In a short distance we spotted the ruins of several ancient coke ovens. I was disappointed that no one had taken the time or effort to post a sign about these old picturesque structures. All I could do was imagine men working feverishly stoking these hot ovens with pieces of tree limbs to heat coal to a high enough temperature to produce charcoal from the coal for use in mining or smelting operations.

I checked the Internet for information on Alhambra and a website was available from the Department of Environmental Quality. It stated that three mines operated near town in the Prickly Pear Creek area. They were called Carbonate Chief, Bell, and Mockingbird Mines. The Internet said that gold, silver, lead, and copper ore were mined and that by 1907, almost one million dollars of material had been dug out of the nearby hills. A Yuba dredge was brought to Alhambra in 1938. It sounded like that was close to the time that the mines shut down. The coke/charcoal processing was not mentioned.

**ANACONDA, MT,** is about twenty miles west of Butte. It is off I 90 and onto Highway 1 for a short distance. The most distinctive feature of the city is the 585 ft. tall smelter smoke stack. The outside diameter is 86 ft. You can see it from the Interstate.

According to Patrick Morris in his book Anaconda Montana, the beginning of the city started way back when Marcus Daly invested in a mine in Butte that was rich in both silver and copper. It was called the Anaconda Mine. Daly contacted George Hearst, the newspaper millionaire for financial backing in 1881 because ore needed to be processed in a smelter and Butte did not have the available water for one. The Warm Springs Creek west of Butte met this need. Daly's friend Morgan Evans helped him buy land for the smelter and the town of

Anaconda began.

At its peak of operation, 1,200 men worked at the smelter in Anaconda. Eventually a refinery was built, too. Daly's company was called the Anaconda Copper Mining Company. He was concerned about housing for his workers and he had rows of houses erected in 1887 a short distance away. This little town took on its own name: Carroll.

Over the years of operation the first smelter site was called Old Works. Later it was demolished and the next worksite was called Washoe Works. About this time the smelter was producing eight million pounds of tailings a day!

These statistics from Matt Kelly's book Anaconda, Montana's Copper City show the immense production of the smelter by the Anaconda Reduction Department in 1955 such as 252 million pounds of copper and huge amounts of zinc, manganese, and super phosphate.

Outside the mining industry, Mr. Kelly told about Marcus Daly's investment of almost five million dollars producing the Anaconda Standard newspaper. He hired editors from Syracuse, N. Y., and artists from back east and he bought expensive linotypes like ones used in big cities. At one time this paper attained 20,000 addresses in its circulation.

Another eye-opener about Anaconda that Matt Kelly stated in his book were facts taken from the 1896 city directory: there were listed 20 lawyers, 15 doctors, 58 saloons, 13 tailors and many more businesses to give an idea of this up-to-date town in Montana!

Marcus Daly brought a special interest in horses and horse racing to Anaconda and the surrounding area. He had unique grooming barns and jockeys at his Hamilton, Montana, farm for his best horses that he entered in races far from here. His favorite horse was Tammany. This horse won a race in 1892 in New York with a $3,000 bet by Daly. Later an artist was hired from an eastern state to inlay hardwood pieces on the floor of the Montana Hotel with a design of Tammany's head. They said that no one wanted to step on that part of the room.

Mr. Daly had a great deal of influence on people in the town of

Anaconda. I had read that he had a more personal interest in the smelter workers and their families than some of the other "Copper Kings". Years ago there was an all-day picnic for the whole family and it was called Smeltermen's Day. Now early in August, the town holds Marcus Daly Days with a children's parade, an ice cream social, and other outdoor activities.

Anaconda has some very interesting places to visit. The Copper Village Museum and Arts Center is in the old city hall. We toured it in 2010 and found it to be very nice. That is where I bought Anaconda books by Matt Kelly and Patrick Morris.

Our Montana Ghost Town Conference in 2011 was centered around the history of both Anaconda and Phillipsburg. Our Conference leaders arranged for us to tour the Washoe Theatre here on Main Street. It was built in 1936 and still operates today. The original tall drapes and ceiling designs have been preserved. There are several very old beautiful churches in Anaconda, a Carnegie library, and the Copper Village museum and art center.

Today most of the old masonry foundations, iron litter, slag, and tailing piles have been cleaned up. The Washoe Park was developed near the smelter stack as a tribute to the very historic site where the Washoe Works smelter operated up until 1980.

The Old Works Golf Course was built over the old slag piles in 1997. It is an 18 hole golf course designed by Jack Nicklaus. The construction required pouring thousands of cubic yards of soil over the black surface. It is quite impressive. Our Conference meetings and banquet were held at the Clubhouse and it was very pleasant. There are walking trails surrounding the golf course and I took advantage of that for my early morning walks.

Summer bus tours are available for Anaconda's visitors. You sign up at the Chamber of Commerce headquarters on East Park by the old caboose and train depot.

BANNACK, MT, is located west of Dillon, MT, on Highway 278. It was one of our favorite mining towns and one of the best organized as far as having all of its thirty-plus buildings labeled. Part of the reason for this is because it is designated a Montana State Park. Obviously, this allows some funding for its maintenance. We visited this great ghost town in 2001, 2005, and 2009. A nice museum/gift shop greats you as you enter the premises. One of the most striking edifices is Hotel Meade, which has been restored nicely. I have read that a ghostly Halloween party is planned by the Bannack Association in the Meade Hotel in recent years. Two of the other large structures are a beautiful old Methodist Church and a Masonic Lodge. A wooden walkway runs along in front of most of the town's buildings and there is a little numbered post in front of each one. A free brochure in the gift shop is a guide for the post numbers explaining what each house or business was originally.

Bannack was the first territorial capital and its territorial governor was Sidney Edgerton. (My grandkids' elementary school was named after him.) Bannack was not a capital very long. The Edgertons did not live in the Meade Hotel. They had their own one-story house nearby, according to a photo caption printed in 1864. On the negative side of Bannack's history, it was here that Sheriff Henry Plummer was hanged for his schemes of setting up robberies of miners carrying gold. It was thought that possibly 100 miners were robbed and killed by the Plummer gang before the self-elected justice team of Vigilantes put a stop to these heinous crimes. In the past years a few authors have showed some skepticism about the guilt of some of the men who were hanged without much investigaton or trials.

"Bannack Days" is held on the third weekend of July each year. (For exact dates, check the Bannack website.) Our last two trips from Billings to this great ghost town was for that event. The first trip over was an impulsive act on my part. Three days before the weekend dates of Bannack Days, I was reading a Montana Magazine and saw a notice for it. I hopped up, found Dave somewhere in the house or garage, and told him I wanted to go because we didn't have plans for the weekend yet. I offered him a deal: if we could find a motel room at Dillon, we would drive over early on Saturday, stay over, and take in the Sunday activities at Bannack, too. He agreed. I got out my Montana Gold West Country tourist guide and found the Dillon motels. (No, we didn't have Internet at that time!) In no time, I booked us a motel and we started making our plans for the drive Sat. We were so happy that we went. There were many people attending, some of them in Western costumes. They had old-fashioned bluegrass bands playing in several locations in Bannack. There were a number of "hands-on" activities such as making candles, shooting a black powder rifle, searching a rock pile for garnets, watching a miner's stamp mill operate, making candles, etc. The Dillon community clubs sold lemonade, burgers, popcorn, etc. and a few buildings were opened for the sale of ice cream, lace parasols, metal sculptures, or other Montana-made products. Parking was set up to accommodate dozens of cars. The state park staff and volunteers kept everything on schedule and helped visitors find their places of interest. The highlight of the two days was the real-live dramas of " shoot outs" over card games and a stagecoach hold-up with live horses and the actors all in costume. On the porch of the Hotel Meade was a debate about whether or not women should be allowed to vote. The visitors could participate by hollering out their objections or pros. A man dressed as a judge was heading up the discussion. Of course, Dave grinned at me and shouted out reasons against women voting! I got so sunburned that Saturday but it was worth the pain.

A funny thing happened at the 2009 Bannack Days. Dozens of us attendees were lined up on both sides of the upper road that runs perpendicular to the town's main street. All of us were waiting for the stagecoach and horseback riders to come down the hill into Bannack. It was hot , the melodrama was running late, and everyone was showing a little impatience. An attractive woman dressed as a "bar-room hostess" approached Dave and me and we were joking with her. In a minute, she reached down in her high-heeled boot and pulled out a small Derringer gun! She spoke up loudly, "No one crosses me!" and she laughed.

Shortly afterward, another actor approached dressed in black pants, a nice long-sleeved dress shirt with garters above his elbows, and a nice black Stetson. We started joking with him and asking questions to pass the time. He came up really close to me and suddenly unbuttoned the front of his shirt. He pulled back both sides of the shirt. Mounted against the skin of his chest was the most authentic-looking plastic eyeball!! He grinned at me and said, "I've got an eye on you, Lady!" We all roared with laughter as they all observed his chest ornament.

On July 30, 2012, the Billings Gazette printed an article about a company called Dutch Gold Resources Inc. and Trelis Corp. that has started bulk-sampling work along Grasshopper Creek four miles from Bannack. They hope to mobilize equipment in the fall of 2012. They would operate under a "small miner exclusion" rule that is for small scale operations and has less restrictions from state environmental review. We will see how this "pans out"!

In July of 2005, we drove off Interstate 90 to explore the little town of BASIN, MT. It is north of Butte. Basin had three active gold mines years ago. One was called the Katy and another was Hope Mine. Later the men excavated the two mines underground until they were joined. Then it was renamed the Katy-Hope Mine. The third mine was called the White Elephant. About 1924 the company operating here was named Jib Consolidated Mining Co. Mounds of mining materials on hillsides in several directions can be seen from the streets in Basin.

For some time now two radon mines have given an economic boost to some of the small businesses. People buy groceries, rent motels, cabins, or bring R. V.s to this little berg for a week's time as they make daily trips to one of the mine's caverns for exposure to its walls of radon. They believe that the radon gas relieves their aches and pains from arthritis or similar ailments. Is this an oxymoron with the public service announcements warning us against harmful radon in the foundations of our homes? We asked people there about the danger of exposure to radon, but they said that these regular visits to Basin were very beneficial.

An older man who lived in Basin named Noel Rinesmith was in his yard as we drove past. Dave got out of our car and asked him if he knew any local history. He invited us into his home and shared some of his experiences of living in Basin for many years. He showed us a huge volume he owned on western ghost towns. I took down the title and author for future reference.

A distinctive feature in the skyline of Basin is a tall brick smoke-stack built for a smelter operation years ago. We also saw an old stone jail still standing.

**BRANDON, MT.** is found out of Sheridan,MT three miles east and up the Mill Creek Road. Also on the Mill Creek Road the ghost town of Smuggler is found. The distinctive feature here is a set of tall stone posts that mark the entrance to this old town. Most of the original buildings have been repaired and re-roofed for summer cabins. Further up the hill is the Toledo Mine. It is adjacent to a well-marked mine called the Tamarack. A good-sized head frame standing over a mine shaft rests in the field. We were told that it was the mining hole for the Toledo. We heard a wild tale that men carried out thin layers of shiny gold in their arms from this mine.

The book Montana Pay Dirt recorded the fact that two other gold mines operated near Brandon. One was the Buckeye and another was called the Broadgauge. In the same book author Wolle quoted the Montana Post newspaper of January, 1865, saying that Brandon had "twenty-seven good log houses, two blacksmith shops, one hotel, and many more buildings under construction."

A number of buildings from the past are still being used as homes here. An old red brick schoolhouse has become a residence. As we ex-plored the town, we got acquainted with a gentleman named Wesley Elser. He was walking around in his yard on this beautiful summer morning and we stopped to inquire of any historic knowledge. Dave walked over to him and struck up a conversation. Mr. Elser said that he had lived in Brandon almost his entire life. I suspect he was in his eighties.

He showed us the concrete foundations of several old buildings and told us that the house across from him was a "remodel" over a very old homestead. It was one of the original Brandon homes, probably the residence of a miner or mine superintendent.

Our conversation was cut short when Mrs. Elser called our new friend into the house to eat his breakfast!

The two **BRANHAM LAKES** are found out of Sheridan, Montana. A person needs to locate the Mill Creek Road and drive about twelve miles on a very rough road going up a small mountain. It is very wise to use a four-wheel drive pickup. We drove there in 2009 and were told by more than one person in Sheridan that the area up the hill was very beautiful. There have quite a bit of rainfall because of the elevation. That summer the hillsides were lush with foliage and covered with both evergreen and deciduous trees. When we arrived at the top of the hill, we were delighted to see the two lakes—small, but fresh looking with a deep bluish hue. There were very nice camping spots with fire pits and a concrete restroom. Walking trails led around the perimeter of one lake

On the drive up to Branham Lakes, we saw a number of mine sites. There were tailings around the Tamarck and the Toledo Mines and a large head frame in the distance from the Buckeye Mine. There was an old ghost town called Smuggler with an entrance of rugged stone pillars and quite a few buildings remaining from the mining days.

We stayed overnight in our pickup camper and woke up to a breath-taking view of the sun shining on the lake in front of us. There are rugged mountains right above you in two directions. I would highly recommend a visit to this scenic area. If you go, be sure to pack a lunch. You'll want to spend several hours there hiking around the woods. I never heard anyone say if the lakes are stocked with trout. We saw only a few other visitors to this scenic place over the two days we were there.

**BUTTE, MT.,** cannot be called a ghost town by any means, but it has a fascinating history of mining that became world renowned for its copper mines and smelters. The wealth made by the famous "Copper

Kings"—William Clark and Marcus Daly in particular— from the many caverns beneath the city affected lives all across the United States. These men used their wealth to buy votes (YES), famous racehorses, mansions in several cities, and made investments all over Montana as well as other states. They touched the lives of working miners from dozens of other countries. Copper Camp, a Writers Project book, is a fun read about the many colorful characters and stories of the city in its prime. When the copper was discovered and the mining started, Butte grew from about 5,000 people to almost 50,000 in just a few years. One book said that with this big population and very few housing accommodations, some hotels rented a sleeping room for only 8 hr. max. They could rent that same bed three times in a 24 hr. time period! I doubt if the bedding got changed after each man.

I have to mention that there was a little corruption in this city years ago. On the underground tour that is offered in Butte, we saw the tunnel that led from the city police offices directly underground to the "speak-easy" bar during prohibition days. The officers could get their illegal booze without the public's notice! If you've read book I or II of Speaking Ill of the Dead – Jerks in Montana History by Dave Walter, Jon Axline, and Jody Foley, you noticed that quite of few of those jerks were from Butte. The Anaconda Copper Mining Company basically ruled the town of Butte and the miners' lives. The local newspapers were only allowed to print articles that were slanted in favor of the "Company". A sad, but humorous story in a Butte paper stated that local ladies had such beautiful dainty complexions. The real fact is that the arsenic in the air coming from the fumes of the smelters was making people's skin pale!

The author Muriel Wolle's books gave some interesting statistics about Butte. She said that before 1882, 80% of U. S. copper came from mines near Lake Superior, but five years later Butte's copper output surpassed the Great Lake copper production. Also she stated that as of 1898, Butte was producing about 41% of the world's copper!

There are actually two very old towns incorporated into Butte. They are Centerville and Meaderville. Both of them were in the northern part of town. Today many of the houses left from these communities are needing repairs, new roofs, and paint. We searched and asked questions of several people to help us find the division between Butte and the two towns. We found one storefront displaying the name Centerville and three that were labeled Meaderville. I think they have both lost their identities.

Dave and I grew to love Butte for its colorful past and its friendly locals. We stayed at the Copper King Mansion several times under the owners' warm hospitality. Another picturesque structure in Butte is the Charles Clark Chateau, built for him by his father William Clark. It is now an art gallery. The city has a number of huge beautiful churches. Many of them are Catholic because of the predominance of Irish people in Butte. The World Museum of Mining on the campus of the college has excellent specimens of rocks and minerals from around the world. The biggest piece of amethyst I've ever seen is there. One of my favorite book stores in the state is Second Edition is in Butte. It's a little cluttered, but it has a huge variety of books, and real bargains, and friendly owners/clerks. The old Finlen Hotel is worth visiting. We stayed there in September, 2008, during our Montana Ghost Town Preservation Society conference. I guess the Finlen owners used postcards showing the beautiful chandeliers hanging from the ceiling and the intricate features of the giant pillars in the main lobby and worked at restoring the hotel back to its original design.

One of our favorite stops in Butte was Pork Chop John's for their famous pork sandwiches. When Tom Orizotti was headed to Billings for one of his daughter's school events, he would call Dave and ask if he should bring us a case of pork fritters. We were there for St. Patrick's Day festivities and Evel Knievel Days, but, believe it or not, we did not drive to Butte for either of these events. In 2001 we were driving back from seeing our son's family in Portland. We left the interstate to get lunch in Butte and came to a street lined with crowds of people sporting lots of green hair and raffia and realized it was March 17! The parade had just finished. We were lucky to even find a place to eat. We observed Evel Knievel Days in 2010 on a trip back from Missoula where we and our son's family all rode our bikes on the old railroad bed called the Hiawatha Trail. This time also we had planned to just run into Butte for a quick lunch stop and had not kept track of when the Evel Knievel Days were held. You would think that we live in a vacuum! We found streets blocked off with food vendors tents and tables and one street piled high with gravel for young men to ride up to the top of the mound and do flips in the air. The town was flooded with motorcycles and crowds of spectators. We joined right in and watched the action. It proved to be fun observing the extremes of tattoo art on body parts and seeing every size and shape and age of men and women in leathers, wild hairdos, and a few people there like us, just enjoying the sights.

CANYON CREEK CHARCOAL KILNS are neither mines nor a ghost town, but a very significant site involving the mining process. They are located south of Butte on I 15. Drive past Divide to Melrose and follow the signs to Glendale and straight ahead to the kilns. These round brick ovens remind you of giant beehives in shape! The remains of twenty-five kilns still stand today. Years ago we tried to reach them, but the road was too rough for our car. This time in July of 2009, we drove our 4-wheel drive pickup and made it fine. The road was much better and a new sign had been added for distance to the special historic site and at the location of the kilns several new sign boards were posted for public knowledge. From these markers we learned that logs were piled inside clear to the top of the ovens and burned twenty-four hours a day continuously for over two weeks to produce a good grade of charcoal. The signboard said that when the charcoal was cooled, it was loaded on wagons and pulled by horses to the smelter at Glendale, about six miles away. One outstanding statistic on the signboard read: In the year 1895 at the peak of kiln usage, three square miles of trees were felled and brought to these coke ovens by horse and wagons. This area would be in the Beaverhead Forest. Dave had me stand beside one of these kilns for a photo to show the size of structure. It was easily five times my height!

CHARTER OAK Mine that operated out of Elliston, MT from the 1890s until the 1960s was at its peak in the 1940s. We had a tour guide to this mine—: Mr. Terry Beaver, a retired teacher and Forest Service employee who we met through a Helena friend, Rich Armstrong.

Mr. Beaver told us that several generations of one family, the Bonners, worked the mine and mill for many years, but had never registered the claims on the land. In World War II lead and zinc were in high demand and Charter Oak was in full operation extracting these two ores plus silver and gold. Of course, this benefited the family and its employees greatly. Some years later, dead fish were discovered in the Little Blackfoot River which lies downhill from this mine. This was likely from pollution of the area's water. Rather than paying the cost of reclamation and removing cadmium and other chemicals from the region, the mine owners walked away from their mining interest.

The U. S. Forest Service stepped in at this point, took over the mine property and paid for the reclamation project. This was about 1995. A reclamation decision was made to restore all these mine buildings and the mill as an educational facility.

Terry Beaver took us through each area of the mine operation, but not into the seven adits (mine tunnel entrances). He told Dave and me about the work inside the mine also: —how drilling was done, how dynamite was used, etc. He shared with us that miners were given three candles on each shift because three of them lasted the twelve hours. He said later carbide lanterns were introduced. There was a "sample" lunch pail on display in one room. It was made in layers for each part of the meal.

Mr. Beaver stated that in early days most men's wages were only about fifty cents a day; whereas, miners were paid three dollars and fifty cents a day, so these jobs were in high demand.

Electricity came to Charter Oak Mine in 1939. A big breakthrough followed in mining methods. They were able to mechanize the mine and mill. Big pneumatic drills and compressors were installed. In the mill conveyor belts could move the ore from one processing area to another. Also electric motors for the ball mill could more efficiently operate crushing processes inside the huge canisters. All these were good labor-saving devices for the miners.

One amazing thing we saw on display was inside the mill:—four flotation cells for removing specific types of valuable ore. Each tub contained different chemicals or products for its use. One was to retrieve gold. Each cell had the capability of floating specific minerals, which required the use of xanthates. This required an amalgamation of the desired mineral while creating an hydrophobic mixture. The amalgam was similar to the attraction of mercury to gold or salt to silver. Another one was to retrieve lead and they used sodium ethyl xanthate, if I heard it correctly. I was taking notes as we walked around.

Terry Beaver said that the name Charter Oak came from the Bonner family history. They had lived in the Hartford, Connecticut area where oaks were commonly grown. The British were asking for each colony's charter and supposedly, one was hidden in an oak tree away from the Brits. The story goes that in 1750 the oak with the hidden charter was struck by lightning and the tree died. Locals salvaged the tree and made special wooden keepsakes from that charter-oak!

Our tour lasted several hours. We walked all over the grounds and inside many buildings where we also viewed a jaw crusher, a Grizzly classifier, the Regent House where chemicals were stored, and the Assay office. In the back woods we saw a number of other pieces of equipment lying "in a bone yard" in among the trees. Many of the buildings and items inside them were labeled with nice steel signs.

Dave and I were very thankful for this great educational tour, quite an opportunity to learn more about our passion: — Montana's mining history!

COMET, MT, had a former owner who was very upset about vandalism to his buildings so he posted a stiff warning about not harming them anymore. I think he also tried to keep this ghost town location off the Montana maps. In 2005 we headed in the direction that a western book described, but we had driven quite a few miles with no sign of Comet. About that time, we met a vehicle coming toward us and we stopped, hoping that the driver might help us. An elderly couple was inside the old pickup. When Dave asked about Comet, the man replied that yes, indeed, he knew where it was—a few more miles on this same road. To our surprise, he also said that he and his wife were the last and only residents of the town!

We proceeded on and in a short time came upon Comet. It had over twenty buildings and a huge mill up on a steep hillside. Some of the buildings were just piles of boards, but a few were in better shape. A couple houses were two-storied structures, possibly a hotel or mercantile store. We drove up the hill the opposite direction from the mill and could view the whole array of buildings below. That is when we spotted a long mobile home in among the old buildings. We decided that must be the residence of the couple we met on the road a short time ago. Both of us really liked this ghost town.

In September of 2006 we traveled back to Comet in our car, guiding our Texas cousins Fred and Connie Bernhardt in their pickup with a Lance camper on top. Fred grew up in Montana and they shared our interest in old ghost towns. The four of us walked around the old structures, peering in, but not daring to walk on old rickety floors or under sagging roofs, and always watching for signs of snakes. We took photos everywhere, especially Fred. We decided to cross the rocky creek bed and climb the hill to the stately mill—still standing because of its sturdy metal roof. We peeked in at the huge, open room of the mine building. Some machinery stood where it had been operating years ago, rusting and falling apart. Old ladders and unstable-looking stairs led to the floor above. We didn't dare take a chance to climb them and observe the upper level…All the side doors but one were open and inviting. In one room about fifty bags of cement mix or powdered chemicals were piled one on top of another in a corner, misshapened by time.

As dark set in, we realized that we wanted to take more pictures and we had lost our daylight. We talked it over and decided we could sleep in our car with a spare blanket from the trunk, our extra coats, and some close snuggling! Fred and Connie were fine in their big camper. We slept fairly well. Only one car of teenagers drove past late at night and two cows wandered through the road near us.

Early the next morning, Fred rapped on our Chevy window and asked us to come into their camper for some fresh coffee.—so delightful in the cool morning mountain air! Connie had deli rolls and a choice of cereals and we were ready to explore Comet more as soon as the sun came up enough for good photos. We left Comet with a special respect for the great little mining camp that it had been when the big mill was operating and men were busy working right where we stood.

COULIDGE OR COOLIDGE, MT., is south of Anaconda close to Wise River and the frequently-advertised Crystal Park where you can freely search for crystals in the earth.

Signs lead you to Coolidge, but you will need to walk a couple miles to see all the buildings left in this ghost town. As we walked down the road toward the mill, it was as though we were just going down the main street of an old, old town. Almost all the structures were on one side of the road. A few houses were in decent shape. My opinion is that because the area is so full of trees, then the wood in the buildings does not dry out as much as those ghost towns that rest in hot sun. We got to see the huge old mill in 2001. It sat across a small stream of water, off to the right. Later we learned that the mill was totally destroyed and hauled away a few years ago.

According to Jack Gilluly in his brochure on Coolidge, the mill was so large that it covered two acres.

ELKHORN, MT., was so interesting that we went there in 2000 and took our Texas cousins with us to show them in 2006. The ghost town is found in the hills 12 miles out of Boulder, MT., and it was Dave's favorite, probably. On our 2000 year trip, we had stayed at the Castoria Inn in Boulder. It was a Bed and Breakfast at that time and we had planned to drive back to Billings that morning. Jeff and Bev Jones, the owners of this beautiful castle-like house, were visiting with us in their front yard and told us about Elkhorn and directions to go there. To think what we would have missed! Somewhere I read that William Jennings Bryan delivered his Cross of Gold speech here. One western book stated that $14,000,000 of silver was mined from the hills of Elkhorn.

The old Fraternity Hall of Elkhorn still stands out as the most frequently photographed building of all the ghost towns. I have yet to do a decent watercolor of the building to get the proper dimensions of the protruding wooden face plate. Elkhorn has a very large and interesting cemetery on a hillside above the town. We were told that the many graves of young children were deaths from a diphtheria or a flu epidemic. Some headstones had lambs or angels on them.

There are a lot of buildings in Elkhorn and an interesting huge water tower made of wooden slats with metal straps going around it. A few of the old buildings are labeled and there is now a signboard giving some historic facts about Elkhorn. Because much of the Elkhorn property is privately owned, some of these people have chosen to remove their buildings from the town, but we never learned the reason. It has certainly been disappointing to some of us history buffs.

THE EMPIRE MINE existed near Marysville, MT. We had talked to a man working in his yard in Marysville and he gave us directions, but we never found any signs on the road. The way in was rough and steep and curved much of the way. After quite a few miles, Dave drove our pickup over one hill and found ourselves right beside small fenced-in areas of land that had metal signs labeled "DANGER MINE SHAFT". When we stopped the truck to look down in the holes, they were very deep and anywhere from six to eight feet across. We had not intended to go near any more of these deep holes, but we could not turn around anywhere so we had to continue forward, with me almost holding my breath since I do not like places like this.

After we passed the fifth shaft, the rocky road started going downhill and we were relieved to see a clearing ahead. Lo and behold, there was a man clearing trees and brush on a small Ford tractor with a blade on the back of it. We stopped the pickup and walked over to visit with him. We explained that we were amateur historians, searching for history, not minerals, and we had just gotten off a hilly road and might be lost.

He quickly explained that we were indeed on Private Land—his! As we talked more, he relaxed and was less defensive. He introduced himself as the land owner and stated that he had been buying land in this Empire mine area and was selling lots for summer cabins and had also built cabins on a couple lots and was offering them for sale with the property.

We apologized for driving on his land without permission. He said that he was curious about the old diggings left from the Empire and had posted the signs to protect the public from a cave-in. He also stated that he had climbed down several of the mine shafts himself to see what had been done by the former mine owner. That sounded scary to me if he had fallen or gotten hurt and would be a long way from an ambulance or sheriff.

We thanked him for the information and realized that there were no longer any cabins or physical evidence of the Empire mine except the mine shafts. This man had probably razed them for his real estate enterprise.

## GATES OF THE MOUNTAINS

This title is the name given to a natural waterway of the Missouri River that narrows and curves. Meriwether Lewis named this location back in the early 1800s on his expedition through Montana. The direction is north of Helena about 15 miles on Highway 15. A local business provides daily boat trips here during the summer months. The tour takes about two hours.

The scenery in the area is very pretty. When you leave the wide part of the Missouri River and move into the canyon, rugged cliffs rise up on both sides of the river. A guide tells you to watch for wildlife along the way. The boat makes a stop at a landing for people to take a break and learn about more history of the area. The Mann Gulch tragedy took place close by in 1949. A bronze plaque tells about how firefighters lost their lives up on the hillside during a forest fire..

We took this boat tour twice and thoroughly enjoyed the beautiful scenery. It was well worth the cost of the river cruise.

To find the town of GLENDALE, you go north of Dillon and turn off at Melrose. Glendale still has a huge stone smokestack used in its forty ton copper ore smelter many years ago, in the 1890s. The framework of the mill building made out of local rock is still somewhat intact. It had amazing hand-laid stonework

In 1878 Glendale had a population of 950. A newspaper called the Atlantis was printing and circulating papers at that time. A few of our history books have quotes from this paper. Hecla Consolidated Mining Company ran the smelter and blast furnaces for over twenty years.

From our study and visit to the Canyon Creek charcoal ovens several more miles further on this road, we learned that the supply of charcoal was produced in those ovens and hauled by horse and wagons here to Glendale for this smelter. I can just imagine the busy activity of men working here all those years ago!

In 2004 we went in search of GOLD CREEK, MT., one of Montana's first gold discovery sites. The ghost town is near Anaconda right off I 90 with a green highway sign for help. A small solid concrete pillar that is painted light green rests near the local post office. This post says 1866-1966,—a one hundred year milestone marker for the little town.

Signs on the highway advertise the Gold Creek Overland Stage rides, but our schedule did not allow us to take that ride. We spotted their little base of the business as a separate house in Gold Creek set off by itself to the west of the town's other buildings.

Most of our history books talk about this area as one of the first gold discoveries in the state. Granville and James Stuart and another man named Benetese did find gold here of good quality, but the mining prospects were short lived. The town of Pioneer rests nearby, but sits on private land.

In September of 2006 we tried to tour GOLDEN SUNLIGHT Mine

which is almost directly north of Cardwell, Mt. We were traveling in two vehicles with our Texas cousins, Fred and Connie Bernhardt. We learned a little bit about the mine after talking to the owner of Calico Pottery because her father had worked there years ago.

We decided to leave their pickup/camper there at Cardwell and all four of us rode up the mountain in our car to ask about a tour. Dave found a mine supervisor. The foreman on shift was very polite and said that sometimes they do give tours, but the mine runs 23 hours a day and they were in the process of a shift-change and no one was free to lead a tour.

Another man had overheard our conversation and said that he was an electrical engineer for Golden Sunlight. He pointed to several huge buildings, some of them shaped like giant cylinders with cone roofs. He gave us a brief summary of the basic process working there. He told us that Barrick Company owns gold mines around the world. He stated that ore is ground down three times until it is powder. They also use cyanide for chemical changes and magnetic action that causes the gold to adhere to sponge-like bars. The gold is removed, melted, and later made into bricks. Before we left, he gave us a brochure about Golden Sunlight with phone numbers to call for a tour sometime in the future.

Dave and I really wanted to visit Golden Sunlight up close and personal, so finally in July of 2010 after several calls, we made an appointment to get a mine tour on a Friday morning. We left Billings at 5:00 A.M. to make sure we were plenty early. After a cup of coffee at the Cardwell store, we headed up the mountain. We checked in at the "out post" where a young lady took our names, made some phone calls and then we were asked to watch a twenty minute video on mine safety and information on Barrick Co. that owns Golden Sunlight. She gave us hard hats and bright-colored vests and we were ready to go. Our first tour guide was Zeke who had us ride in a company extended-cab pickup. He drove us up to the top of the mountain and we were amazed to look down into a huge pit, almost the same as the Berkeley Pit in Butte. He explained how the earth has been cut out in layers to remove ore and dumped into huge trucks many times larger than ones I've seen on construction sites. Of course, the trucks haul the earth up out of the pit to the mill operation above.

The second phase of our mine education was a walking tour guided by the mill superintendent Rick. He took us into a conference room and used illustrations to show us what we would be observing under his direction. We walked all over the plant and saw the rod mill, the ball mill, the cyanide pond, and finished off with a visit to staff in the lab-testing rooms.

Both of the tour guides to Golden Sunlight Mine emphasized the need for safety and also that EPA often checks on this mine's operations for proper care of ore waste products to prevent pollution to ground water, etc. The Billings Gazette said in 2012 this mine asked the government to allow them to enlarge their pit by 4,000,000 tons of ore for processing.

GRANITE, MT., sits about 7 miles up the hill from Philipsburg. This silver mine was very productive in its peak years. It had many buildings,:—a Union hall, saloons, fraternity lodges, banks, and even a hospital. According to several of our western history books, the mine superintendent, Mr. Weir, and other top officials all had stone houses laid out down one street. It was called "Silk Stocking Row" because of the mine officials wives' fine clothing who lived in those houses. Some of the stone foundations of those houses can still be seen in Granite today and the framework of the Union hall building is still standing. It was also in stone. The majority of the other structures were wooden, so there is very little remaining of them.

A great deal of the mill foundation in the shape of a multi-level terrace of hand-laid rock remains intact after all these years. I was excited to see the heavy wood timbers that were the base for the tram running down the hill through the trees. In a couple places we saw pieces of the thick steel cable resting on some of the A-framed trestle stands for the tramway. The tram brought ore cars down the hill to the smelter from Granite to Rumsey that sits on the edge of Philipsburg.

In July of 2010 we arrived at Granite after a rough road up the hill, we three decided to get out of the pickup to stretch our legs. (My mother was on this ghost town trip with us.) No sooner had we left the truck when Dave yelled out, "There's a bull moose!" It must have been resting in the shade of the stone wall of the mill. As we made haste for the truck, we saw a second moose, a female, get up and stand. She had been in the shadows right behind the male.

We left the area of the mill and explored more of the Granite premises. As we went closer to the far end of town, we could hear pounding in the distance. Dave drove toward the sound and in a short time, we saw a man up on a ladder leaning against the wall of an old building nailing up a board. We stopped and asked him about his project on the structure. He explained that he was from the University of Montana at Missoula. He was doing some restoration work on a building here in Granite funded by a grant from the college for historic buildings. We thanked and encouraged him for his labor and told him about the moose across town. We were really glad to see work done on this special old ghost town.

On our drive down the hill leaving Granite, we met another vehicle coming up the road. It was a nice lady who we learned was the wife of the man doing the restoration work. She said that she planned to do some jogging around Granite and visit her husband. We told her about the two moose near the big mill and suggested that she postpone her outdoor exercise today! She totally agreed and continued up the hill.

JEFFERSON CITY, MT, is a small hamlet south of Helena. It still had its own post office in April of 2006 when we located it. We were exploring ghost towns with our Texas cousins Fred and Connie Bernhardt on this trip. Dave drove right up to the postal building knowing there must be a live person on duty since this was not a weekend. Sure enough, the clerk had a little history about the town's past. She said there had once been a huge gold dredge sitting in the creek bed nearby, and, amazingly, she had a photo of the dredge there in her office! She cordially offered to use the postal copier and quickly made us a nice black and white print. The postmistress told us that the dredge had been disassembled and shipped to South America some time back. The lady suggested that we visit a man named James Madison that lived in a big old white house nearby because he was the local historian.

All of us wasted no time and tramped across the grassy field up to his sidewalk. Fortunately, he was home and very responsive to our inquiries on the past history of Jefferson City. He pointed in the distance and said that there used to be a tall smokestack over there. He showed us a few old buildings in the area and two brick structures of long ago. Then he spoke up abruptly and said, "The thing you really need to see is the big mine currently operating just a few miles away."

He gave us directions and then added a warning—"I don't think they'll shoot you if you enter the grounds!" That was comforting. . .!

We hesitated briefly and discussed the risk. Finally, we thought, "What the heck, we'll take our chances."

We drove up the road to the mine and saw a big sign Montana Tunnels—-Apollo Mine. Dave drove our car right through the gate and up to the door marked Office. A man was right inside the door. He looked busy, but was friendly and listened politely when we asked if we might be able to have a tour of the mine. He said to wait there near the front door and he would check with a supervisor. Another man came out of his office and told us he would be willing to give us a tour, but we would have to wait about one-half hour until he was free.

We visited quietly and took pictures of some of the photo displays on the wall. Shortly afterward, a man named Jeff told us four to get in his big suburban truck for the tour and handed us hard hats to wear. He drove up the hill and stopped frequently to explain the various mining activities going on at each site. They used very impressive big equipment. He told us that they were mining four minerals: gold, silver, zinc, and lead. They had a big ball mill that ground the ore down into small pieces. We were not able to look inside for liability reasons.

Jeff told us that they were reclaiming the land surfaces as they went along. He said that 85,000,000 tons of earth were processed in the mill in an amazing period of time. After about an hour of time, he drove us back to the mine office and we thanked him and left.

LAST CHANCE GULCH of Helena, MT, starts on North Montana Avenue in that city and meanders through downtown for several blocks and ends at Broadway. Urban renewal and new houses changed part of it. It used to go to the junction of Oro Fino Gulch.

My friend Ann Bailly who has lived in Helena for many years told me that gold was discovered here in 1864 and within four years $19,000,000 had been mined from Last Chance Gulch. By 1888 there were about fifty millionaires living in Helena—more than any city in the World (per capita). About that time the name Last Chance was changed to the more sophisticated name of Helena. Reeder's Alley is in this section of the city and is known for its art galleries and "Cutesy" shops (Dave's expression for totally un-masculine places to visit!) At the entrance to this area on North Park there is an old log structure called the Pioneer Cabin. It had been one of the original houses of Last Chance Gulch built by a Mr. Wilson Butts and later added on by his brother Jonas Butts. The second brother lived in this home with his wife and three daughters. Now it is an information center for tourists. A man working there was very helpful with some of the same facts that Ms. Bailly supplied.

Dave did let me visit some of the quaint little shops and tourist at-tractions found here that portrayed Helena's colorful past.

In August of 2009 we finally took time to visit LAURIN (lo ray), Mt., which is on Highway 287 north and west of Virginia City. It was the site of an 1863 gold strike. One distinctive building in this little ghost town is the old red brick Catholic Church called St. Mary of Assumption Church which was built in 1902. When we explored Laurin, several men were up high on scaffolding doing repairs on the building. We went inside and found it to be very nice and well kept, amazing for such a small community.

We found an old boarded-up tavern called the Vigilante. It must have had a lot of patrons in its time to warrant such a long spacious building.

We saw an old school across town and a very huge barn across the street from the church. The size of this barn indicated a fairly prosperous ranch or farm operation. It didn't look like it was used anymore. A modern house nearby appeared to be occupied.

We learned that Laurin was the site for a busy stage stop years ago. A man in his yard answered some questions for us. He pointed out where the stage stop building had been, but absolutely nothing remained there now. He told us that Laurin had a reputation of being quite a wild town long ago. Men would get drunk and ride through town on their horses shooting at anything in sight. Parents kept their children inside most evenings.

Laurin is located near Robbers' Roost, an old hotel used by western outlaws or road agents. It was run by a man named Pete Daly and was a stage station also. The upstairs was a dance hall and the downstairs was a saloon.

LEITERVILLE (pronounced light er vil). MT, is found on the Wisconsin Creek Road out of Sheridan, MT. The background for hearing of this ghost town is quite unusual. Dave and I have been Billings Police Dept. volunteers for several years. One of the police interns, Kayla Broksle, visited with us at work and shared that her parents were caretakers of an old mining town out of Sheridan where she grew up. The landowners lived in another state, so Kayla's folks maintained the cabins and kept the entrance gate locked. She provided her parents' work phone numbers and in July of 2009, we drove to Sheridan to get permission to photograph Leiterville

. We got to Sheridan and visited Mrs. Broksle at the Clinic where she worked. She gave us permission to enter the locked gate by crawling through it and we took off for another ghost town adventure.

We made one big mistake on this trip—we drove our car instead of our pickup. The Wisconsin Creek Road got rockier and rougher the further uphill we drove. When we heard scraping sounds under our car, we parked it beside the road, grabbed our camera and took off walking. We had to hike three miles uphill and finally found the buildings that met the description given us. We climbed through the nice wooden log fence and were thrilled to see so many buildings in fairly good shape. The landowners of Leiterville had replaced roofs on many of the old wooden houses. We had been told that several of them were used for summer cabins. We saw big piles of firewood so it must still be pretty cold there part of the year because of the elevation. We walked all over the grounds observing structures in all kinds of condition. The big mill was totally falling down, but we saw fat, rusty cables from a hoist or tram and several wheels lying on the ground among the layers of downed timber. We could tell that the mill had been multi-leveled. Huge wooden beams still stood upright that must have been the main foundation of the mine mill. Muriel Wolle said in her book Montana Pay Dirt that three mill sites were patented at Leiterville. A cyanide plant for testing the ore had been built here, too.

We walked a distance of an acre or so several directions from the restored cabins. There were more than a dozen other buildings scattered out over the forested area. Many of these were in very bad shape and hard to tell their original size.

As we headed back through the log fence, we noticed that the grounds were nicely groomed, no doubt by the caretaker and friends who stay in the cabins in fair weather.

On September 12, 2006, Dave and I wanted to find **MAMMOTH, MT.** We were exploring Montana history with our Texas cousins Fred and Connie Bernhardt in our two different vehicles. All four of us had toured the Apollo Mine, visited Wickes, Elkhorn, and stayed overnight on the grounds of Comet. Now we were at Cardwell studying a map to find South Boulder Road. We located it and decided to leave their pickup and have them ride in our car.

We started down the South Boulder Road and in a few miles, I renamed it Many Boulder Road. It was terribly rocky and rough. We finally found the sleepy little town of Mammoth. It had quite a few beautiful log homes and dozens of summer cottages. We could see only a few historic buildings and old wooden shacks. One hillside revealed reclamation work and up above it appeared to be a couple mine adits (tunnels).

Someone spotted an old stone bank vault with a rusty metal door standing open. We wasted no time getting out of the car to take a closer look and snap a couple pictures of it.

By now it was getting toward supper time and we decided to park in Mammoth beside the main road. Dave and I always carry a cooler on all of our ghost town adventures since we are rarely close to a Hardees or Subway! We spread out our sandwich fixins' and fruit and used the hood of our car for a table.

As we were eating and visiting, a lady stopped her Suburban and walked over. She asked if we had car trouble because she knew that there were absolutely no public services of any kind in this little town. Her name was Kathy Bridges. When we shared our interest in the history of Mammoth, she said that she had framed pictures of the town as it looked years ago on the wall of her cabin and would we like to see them. What a question to ask four historians! She drove off to get the pictures and returned shortly.

We wasted no time viewing them and Fred used his digital camera to take several pictures at different angles to catch a good shot without glare from the glass. Dave did the same with our old 35mm camera.

All of us thanked her and visited more. Connie asked her about her accent and she said that yes, she had lived in Texas:—Plano, Texas. What a coincidence! Fred and Connie had lived there for several years before moving to their present home of Royse City, Texas.

I asked Kathy why the County hasn't repaired the South Boulder Road to Mammoth. She replied that the residents want it left rough so that it keeps people away. They like their quiet little country village. This "quiet life" of Mammoth may have changed now. In the Billings Gazette dated June 23, 2012, Eve Byron of the Independent Record stated that 100,000 tons of tailings have been trucked from this ghost town of Mammoth to the Golden Sunlight Mine north of Cardwell to process in their smelter and extract any gold left in those piles of earth dug out by miners decades ago.

MARYSVILLE, MT., is well marked on Montana maps. It is about 25 miles northwest of Helena. This town has quite a colorful history. A young man from Ireland named Thomas Cruse started as a miner and bought an abandoned claim and kept digging all alone. Eventually he found gold and named it the Drumlummon Mine. He named it after a Catholic parish back home in Ireland. The mine was very productive. It was enlarged to have a multi-level mill. Cruse invested quite a bit of his money from the gold mine into two Helena buildings: the St Helena Cathedral and the foundation of the Montana state capitol. Cruse sold the Drumlummon Mine to an English Company for $1,000,000 plus $500,000 in stock in the mine. In later years Thomas Cruse lost his wife and afterward his daughter both at a young age. In grief and possibly boredom, he invested in another mine, the Bald Butte Mine north of Marysville and was successful there, too.

Today Marysville is a mixture of old churches, stores, and homes sitting alongside modern residences. It appears that the people of Marysville are proud of their past and they have tried to restore some of the structures from its historic days.

In 2011 an article appeared in the Billings Gazette about a company coming into Marysville and starting a renewed interest in mining gold. Dave and I were interested in this news and when we were there recently, we noticed a lot of equipment and men working at one location beside the road to Marysville, so we think that must have been the operation mentioned in the Gazette. Time will tell if the high value of gold will override the cost of the mining industry and make it successful in the future.

A Helena friend reported to me that this recent mining operation is causing some problems to the Marysville residents with heavy traffic on the road that leads to a ski hill and sometimes noisy mining equipment working round the clock.

MAYFLOWER, MT., is south of Whitehall on private land. We made several attempts to see the remains of the ghost town and photograph it, but it was hard to find the owner. Finally, a Billings friend Barbara Wilson made some calls for us and gave us some names to call. Our success came through her friend Roy Milligan who works at the Jefferson County Museum in Whitehall. He had researched Mayflower and written articles about it. We reached him and he kindly found information and old photos at the museum and made copies for us. The day we came to Whitehall which was July 9, 2010, he was out of town, but we picked up the packet he had made for us. Another museum staff member Rucille Shaw helped us also.

The Mayflower owner keeps the gate locked to the road into the mine which lies south of town about three miles. I am choosing not to reveal the owner's name for his privacy. We got permission and found the correct country road. A young man using a swather machine in the field saw us and stopped. We explained our intent to visit Mayflower mine and he asked how long we would be there.

We drove the rest of the way in on the old dirt road and found the remains of the mine operation easily. There was a huge headframe that stood out against the sky, one modern large yellow metal building, and only a couple old wooden houses in the area. This certainly wasn't much left of a mine that William Clark, the Copper King, bought at a price of $150,000 back in 1897 (according to Mr. Milligan's research). Another article at the museum stated that Wm. Clark recovered over $2,000,000 in gold from the Mayflower. One paper said that Clark organized several social events at Mayflower and had special trains bring people to Whitehall from Butte and wagons carry them on into Mayflower. There was even a racetrack over the hill from the mine.

Recent information said that problems with water flooding into this mine have prevented owners from having much success with their mining operations.

We photographed the few structures of Mayflower and drove back down the lane. Right beside the road was a man on a four-wheeler. We stopped to visit and found that he was a brother of the current owner.

He mentioned the water problems at the mine and told us it was a spring and that is why ordinary work with pumps is not always successful. A humorous thing he shared was that a neighbor grew some good potato crops using the water runoff from below the spring.

MIDASBURG and STERLING,MT., are south and west of Norris. They are now on private land and sit very close to each other. Two cousins Tim and Steve Jackson own all the property on which the ruins of these two mining towns rest today. The beautiful stone walls of the stamp mill are barely standing. Already there are gaps in their original framework. Our research stated that this mill employed about ninety men at its prime.

We could see the stonework in the distance as we drove up and parked at the first residence we found. Fortunately, the Jacksons were home on that September day in 2009. Tim Jackson was a rancher/ farmer and his wife taught school in a town nearby. I asked her about my teacher friend who lived in Pony, Janelle Sahr and she knew her, also. Mr. Jackson got into our pickup to go as a guide to Midasburg and Sterling. His cousin who owned the second ghost town wasn't home that day, he said.

We drove up close to the stone structures and found a beautiful old metal plaque on the outside of one natural rock wall. It read: Midas Mill——1867——H. A. Ward, Supt.

The hillside indicated signs of the gold diggings from this mining operation long ago.

My opinion of the stone mill is that an historic organization should get permission from Jacksons very soon and invest money for stone and mortar to reinforce the walls that are decaying from age——before it is too late!

NEVADA CITY,MT., is only two miles from Virginia City We have probably driven through here seven or eight times over the years. Montana State bought the thirty some buildings that comprise Nevada City's outdoor museum from the Bovee family many years ago. A large number of them are set up like a pioneer village now. A reasonable fee is charged to the public to view these historic landmarks. Most of the interiors of the homes and businesses are visible through glass placed across the inside entrance. A visitor can enter the building and view the whole room through the glass.

An old barber shop was moved to Nevada City from Elkhorn, the ghost town near Boulder, MT. Dozens of other homes and businesses are filled with authentic furnishings from Montana's pioneer days. One unique shop is an actual Chinese family business—the building and hundreds of pieces of merchandise on display in their glass display cases including tiny dried fish now covered with layers of dust!

In the summer, a bright-colored railroad engine pulls cars of tourists back and forth between here and Virginia City so that people can visit both cities and view the pretty scenery between them.

In the buildings of Nevada City there is one unique and humorous structure that always draws a laugh:—a two-story outhouse!

PARROT, MT., is found south of Whitehall on Highway 55. You need to watch for Kounty Road and then straight out on that gravel road. To me Parrot is quite a spectacular ghost town because of the massive stone concrete forms covering two levels with a huge difference from the top to the bottom surfaces. The lower section was so large that someone had parked their trailer house in the grassy area between the two parts of that bottom foundation. There must have been about one hundred feet of vertical height for this Parrot smelter.

Another interesting feature that we spotted was out in the field next to the smelter. There stood one good-sized brick oven with an open top, apparently used for making concrete.

As I viewed this big two-story smelter of thick stone, my imagination made me wonder what it must have been like when this mining operation was going full-blast—but, alas! Barbara Fifer researched Parrot for her book Montana Mining Ghost Towns. She said that just before this smelter started operation, Butte's Amalgamated Copper Company started. They sent the ore to the Anaconda smelter and

Parrot's magnificent construction project was never used! Wasn't that a bummer?

PHILIPSBURG, MT., has held me in its spell for many years. We visited there in 2000, 2006, 2009, 2010, and 2011. It is found close to Anaconda. Philipsburg has an amazing number of buildings on the National Historic Register, especially for its size. Dave and I felt that there must be some very civic-minded people and also those who really show a respect for the historic past of Philipsburg to have done all the paperwork that is required to place a building on the National Historic Register.

We noticed that a number of the downtown buildings house businesses that appeal to tourists such as art galleries, gift shops, a sapphire gallery, several nice restaurants, a candy store, etc. It is a fun place to visit.

The big brick school was used much longer than most buildings that old. The elementary school holds the record of the longest, continuously operating school in the state of Montana. (Landusky dropped that title when their school closed several years ago.)

A couple with the last name of Dringle has been working hard to keep productions going in the old McDonald Opera House in the summer with a change of play several times a season. The owners took time to share the history of the opera house and performers of the past.

One thing we really enjoyed was the large museum and book store in Philipsburg. On the last two visits, there were new exhibits that showed a lot of hard work by local historians. The basement is now furnished with authentic full-sized mining equipment displayed like a working mine.

There are three beautiful churches in town that have been maintained nicely, also. There are still a few hundred people living in and around Philipsburg, I would guess.

Philipsburg is surrounded by mining towns—: Granite, Kirkville, Rumsey, and Hasmark being the main ones. Further from town are Maxville, Princeton, Combination, Sunrise, and Black Pine. We visited all of these, but there is very little to see in the last group of mine sites.

If you visit Philipsburg in the summer months, I would suggest that you drive twelve miles west of town on Highway 38 to Gem Mountain—the hands-on sapphire village. You pay for a bucket of gravel and then sift cups of it on a screened wooden frame and dip it into water to look for sapphires. There are Gem Mountain staff walking around to help you do this and to identify any good sapphires. We visited there twice and enjoyed it. Dave surprised me with earrings and a necklace made from some aqua sapphires we found there. He had taken them to a Columbus, MT, jeweler and had them faceted and mounted.

PIONEER, MT., is adjacent to Gold Creek, MT., but a few miles west. Some history books refer to this ghost town as Pioneer City. We learned that Pioneer owners had a dredge that was used all along its river bank. We had heard that it was still intact on private land. We failed to see it in 2004 even though we had learned the name of the land owner. He wasn't home when we stopped.

In 2008 we were able to make contact with the property owner and set up a time to drive from Billings and cross his land and open fences to see this dredge. We followed his directions and walked over a short distance and there sat the huge dredge still resting in a pond of water. Its height was like a two-story house. Sitting out on the end of the digging bar was a big bucket. Considering the age of this great machine, it was still in fairly good shape, probably because the public couldn't vandalize it!

We took lots of pictures. I appreciated seeing one of these monster digging machines up close because we knew several of the mine sites we had visited had had dredges, but all of them were now gone. We did see a section of another dredge sitting in a pond a mile or so from this one. We realized how much work had been done by these dredges by viewing the tons of man-made hills of tailings all around this area. That would have been interesting to watch one of these machines scoop up huge amounts of dirt in its "big mouth".

I couldn't help but think about how much valuable ore is still under those big piles of rock and dirt. With today's price of gold and using modern mining equipment, I think some good profits could be made in re-working these mounds of rock around Montana.

On December 29, 2002, we went to PONY, MT., to see a friend Janelle Sahr who lived there and taught school nine miles away at Harrison, MT. I knew that Pony was on our desired list of ghost towns to visit and I was excited to have a personal guide to the sleepy little burg. Janelle made some calls to get a key to the old two-story brick Pony School and School Gym next door. This allowed us to see the interior first hand. One classroom had been left in its original condition—old school desks with railings on the floor connecting them, textbooks on the shelves, George and Abe's pictures up on the wall, and only a single light on the ceiling. Being an old schoolteacher myself, I loved it. There is a sad thing about these two big school buildings though. They had just been built with optimism that the mining bonanza would continue. They were barely occupied when the local mines closed, the population dwindled, and the school buildings sat empty! Janelle told us that the buildings are sometimes used for community meetings. In the winter the first floor of one building is a "warming house" for ice skaters after they flood the grass outside the building.

We three drove to a family's house, the David Zimmermans, to meet them and buy a book called Pony Homecoming Club written by local residents. The book was better than expected. It was black and white, but it had photos of all the prominent buildings in Pony and a brief history about each one. This family had a unique home and occupation. He made medical prosthetics there in Pony in his own studio. The exterior walls of their home were concrete with the bottoms of colored bottles plastered into the walls. When light shone through them, it gave the appearance of round stained-glass circles. Across town his workshop was built with hay bales used as insulation for all the walls with one bale stacked on top of another vertically inside the stucco interior. Mr. Zimmerman told us that the heating cost for this building was almost zero. Dave was fascinated by both of his personally constructed buildings. We thanked them for allowing us to buy the book all about Pony's history and went on with our tour.

Pony has many summer homes, so its population doubles in warm weather, Janelle told us. There is no longer any school operating in Pony. The children go to school in Harrison nine miles away. Many of the original homes and businesses are quite well preserved we noticed as Ms. Sahr guided us around this town. The Morris State Bank still looks wonderful. It is all brick. A stone wall of the Elling Stamp Mill sits on the edge of town. You can tell that it was a large structure originally. We saw a brick building with words faded but readable on it:—Isdell Mercantile. Our new book on Pony said this store operated from 1885 to 1899. Another prominent brick building was the Mining Office and a block or so from it, you could read REX FLOUR painted on the side of another business. The book said it had been Schreiner's Store in 1901. Across town stood the beautiful old Presbyterian Church established in 1895.

We felt appreciation for this community taking pride in their history and saving so many old historic structures.

We found RIMINI, MT., on July 30, 2004 about ten miles west of Helena off Highway 12. There a sign points to a road going south to Rimini, which is about five miles further.

When we arrived at the little ghost town, there was an obvious controversy between environmental workers doing a huge reclamation project both in the town itself and up the big hill and a second group of people who owned property in Rimini. They had many signs posted up and down the streets telling the public how unhappy they were that the EPA was lifting their homes off their foundations in order to remove contaminated soil.

Dave took a few pictures of some of the old buildings that we thought were left from the mining days. I had ghost town books on my lap researching Rimini. We were debating about driving up the gravel road to see if we could find the old Rimini Mine when a man in a suburban came up beside us and walked over to our car. We shared with him our interest in the history of the area and asked if he knew how to find the mine. He immediately told us not to drive up the hill because the road was very narrow and big trucks were going up and down the hill carrying out loads of contaminated earth from the area of the mine!

He saw the ghost town books on my lap and realized we truly were here for the history, and not here to enter the current conflict of this little town. He explained that he was from Colorado and was the EPA supervisor checking on the reclamation work. Just then he got a call over his "walkie-talkie" from a truck driver up the hill to get permission to come on down. The man with us told the driver to come on down and he looked right at Dave and asked," Do you want to see the reclamation work and the mine area?"

Dave replied "Yes, we'd love to see what's going on."

The supervisor quickly said, "Park your car over there and get into my pickup. A truck's on the way down right now with a load and you have to get out of the road!"

We spent the next hour riding clear to the top of the mountain with the EPA guy. He was a terrific guide with lots of facts and he let us take pictures of the reclamation work! We saw where the top of the mountain had been cut away and had a spectacular view for miles away. He showed us hundreds of new little tree seedlings that had been planted recently on the sides of the hills. There were several large collecting ponds of water that were being treated with neutralizing chemicals to destroy the contaminated substances (probably cyanide) in the water from mining days. What a unique opportunity this was!

I read in a Montana magazine that in World War II, a training camp for military dog sled mushers was established at Rimini in the winter. My friend Ann Bailly told me that Mr. Dave Armstrong of Helena, MT, was one of those mushers and did dog sled races until he was too old to participate.

RUBY, MT., is almost a blink of the eye for size. It is located very close to Virginia City. One of the residents of this little town is Les

Gilman. His family has lived in this area for several generations. We learned about his family's interest in history and that his father Lowell Gilman had written a book called <u>Alder Gulch Remembered</u>. We met Les Gilman in 2009.

We made a phone call to him and set an appointment time to visit his ranch home after he left his office in Sheridan at Ranch Properties. His family has preserved several old buildings like a museum for their historic value from the past. One structure had been the Poor House, a working farm for displaced or unemployed people This enterprise was active back in the 1870s. Les Gilman gave us a tour through the stucco building across from his present home. This building was a shop called a retort where gold was heated in an intense blast furnace, liquefied, poured into molds, and made into gold bricks. A process using mercury was used. Then the mercury was precipitated back into liquid and recycled. Every bit of the original equipment was on display in this retort building, even a harness that a man wore to hide a gold brick next to his chest under his coat! Dave and I were absolutely fascinated and Mr. Gilman was so kind and generous with his time.

Across the farm yard from the retort is a long set of buildings that were constructed for use at the farm when electricity came to Ruby.

All around the area of Ruby are immense numbers of tailing piles left from the gold dredges used to dig up the earth to remove and then process the ore. People told us that recently one or two companies have moved into Alder Gulch, in which Ruby lies, and started using modern mining equipment to extract gold from these mounds of rock. That makes good sense now that the price of gold has risen substantially in the past few years.

The town of Ruby has another distinctive building left from the past:—a beautiful old barn with a faded sign on it which says The Ruby Stables. Of course, the Gilman's historic buildings on their property are the biggest contribution to this little ghost town.

We made two trips from Billings to **SHERIDAN, MT.** in the summer of 2009. Sheridan is not really a ghost town, but definitely full of mining history. We discovered that there were numerous mines in the hills up the Mill Creek Road and the Wisconsin Creek Road. We found out that several stores, a bar, and a hotel in Sheridan's main street all date back almost one hundred years. The stone work on the roof line of the old mercantile store is well preserved. A sign mounted on the store front shows that it is on the National Historic Register.

One thing surprised me in the business district was the very modern all-encompassing hardware store was stationed in the basement of a grocery store!

We visited the Sheridan public library and saw several maps and photos of the town's history. We bought a delightful calendar with twelve black and white photos of past events and people who lived in Sheridan years ago.

On the second trip to Sheridan and Twin Bridges, we took our pickup up the Mill Creek Road on many miles of very rough road surface to reach a destination several people told us we should see:—the two Branham lakes. It was worth the wear and tear on our truck and camper. The scenery was spectacular. There were evergreen trees and wildflowers galore. At the summit where the lakes were, we found hiking trails, a concrete restroom, and fireplaces at each campsite.

Shortly after we arrived, a man from Sheridan drove up with a friend that wanted to see the lakes also. This local man was Tim Nicols and he was interested in western history like us. He shared a few stories about the area and told us that his elderly uncle had reported that he had worked at the Toledo Mine down the hill and actually carried out gold in strips in his arms. It sounded a little far-fetched to me.

We decided that we definitely should stay in our camper here overnight. We gathered wood to make a fire, but "chickened out" when the mosquitos decided to eat us alive! We had insect protection inside and we were still very happy that we stayed overnight because the view of the lakes and the majestic mountains the next morning was breathtaking.

SILVER STAR, MT, is a small town about eleven miles north of Twin Bridges, MT. The most striking feature at Silver Star, the town, is an open air museum of machinery, locomotive engines, an oil derrick, all kinds of mining equipment, and a row of massive iron wheels right by Highway 41. When I saw all this display of equipment, I remembered reading about it and seeing a photo in the book Montana Behind the Scenes by Durrae and Johanek. The owner's name was Lloyd Harkins. He was interviewed by the author of the book. Recently the Montana Quarterly Magazine also featured a story about Mr. Harkins. It said that he had bought many items in Butte in the 1960s when the mines were shutting down. He couldn't bear to see them discarded so he brought them here to his outdoor museum.

On August 23, 2007, we couldn't find anyone around the museum to answer questions. We proceeded to look around Silver Star and noticed a beautiful old brick school, a few businesses, and homes. A gift shop was open on Main Street with some very unique clocks. They had visible gears displaying the working mechanism of the time pieces. Their other artistic items for sale were impressive for this little shop so far from any big city. The area is surrounded by farms and ranches. We drove north past the outdoor museum and a cemetery. Further up the road we saw mine buildings and quite a bit of mining equipment in good shape and as we entered the area, two men in a pickup drove past us toward the structures. We think that the Silver Star Mine may be operating again.

SOUTHERN CROSS, MT., lies close to Georgetown Lake in western Montana. We visited there in 2005. There had been many old cabins from the mining days scattered across the hillside of Southern Cross. We saw piles of boards in the shape of houses lying on the ground. We were walking around studying the old bottles and household items such as metal bedsprings here. About that time, a middle-aged man got out of a car and came to talk to us after we pulled into the area and started hiking around. He told us that a real estate developer found out that the people living in these old homes had basically been "squatters." They did not have deeds to their land or cabins. Most of them were elderly. This man told us that these people were forced out of their homes with nowhere to go because most of them had lived there all their adult lives. He showed emotion on his face about this situation. He said that in 2003 or 2004 the real estate company destroyed all the cabins and subdivided the land to sell lots for people to build summer homes since it was so close to Georgetown Lake and a popular location. Only a few old buildings remained. When we visited further about historic facts, he shared that his aunt was Florence Johnson who had written Ghost Trails Country. We were able to buy that book the following year and it was a very good little paperback with information about mines nearby. Some of the ghost towns or mines were Red Lion, Atlantic Cable, Gold Coin and Hidden Lake. We learned that Gold Coin had a huge ore processing mill. It had been completely demolished shortly before our visit to this area. How sad that an historic site like that is gone.

In 2011 at a Ghost Town Preservation Society conference, I learned that the two last Southern Cross buildings were now owned by St. Timothy's Memorial Chapel that is up the hill from this old ghost town. These structures are the Mine Superintendent's house and the Mine office. Some effort by the church people and historians is being made to preserve them.

TWIN BRIDGES, MT., is south of Whitehall on Highway 41. We traveled there for history reasons in July and August of 2009. The town has quite a few active businesses and friendly people. We discovered that the first hour in town. A lady about our age was sitting on a park bench waiting for her husband. We went up to her and asked about Twin Bridges history. She immediately invited us to a gathering of Senior Citizens at a local restaurant for lunch that very day. She thought that there would be a good chance that some people at this meal could help us. Shortly afterward, her husband joined us and added his invitation. They were Mr. and Mrs. Walter Morris. We walked around town and looked at some of the stores, etc. Later we did go to the Twin Bridges Seniors' luncheon and asked questions of several older gentlemen. They told us about some of the mines in the area and said that in

Sheridan we should drive up Mill Creek and Wisconsin Creek Roads where the majority of the mines were located.

I had some curiosity about the acreage of buildings of the old Children's Orphanage here in Twin bridges. My research led me to read the chapter on it in the book Montana Behind the Scenes by Durrae and Johanek. A few former residents of the orphanage were quoted in this book. It operated over 80 years. It sounds like the children's basic needs were met and some practical life skills were taught, but there was no love given to them. About 6000 youngsters lived there over those years.

We thought the setting of Twin Bridges was very pleasant:—situated in a green, fertile valley surrounded by many ranches and farms. We also will remember the warm welcome we received by the Morris family and the seniors at the restaurant during our visit.

VIRGINIA CITY, MT, is a place of colorful history. It is found south of Three Forks on Highway 87. I had probably been in Virginia City three or four times growing up and once or twice after Dave and I married, but in 1999 and again in 2009 we drove there and truly spent time like a tourist. We went on the trolley tour and were delighted to hear some lively tales of the city's past. We rode up on Boot Hill where notorious criminals were buried and we heard all about the Vigilantes' form of justice. Some of the trials were very brief without much evidence. Quite a number of men were hanged, and recent historians have questioned if all of them were guilty.

We learned that the city was basically owned by the state of Montana since 1997. We spent time in the Thompson-Hickman Museum and the J. Spencer Watkins Museum. The town is filled with a dozen old homes, beautifully restored, and businesses such as the Montana Post, the first state newspaper. The Opera House still produces 19th Century plays in the summer. A Hangman's Building was the scene of five hangings of road agents conducted by the Vigilantes. A visit to the Gilbert Brewing Complex and a drive up to Boot Hill Cemetery should complete your trip here. The town council allows business people to set up shops such as jewelry, baked goods and candy in some of the old main street buildings to keep Virginia City self-sustaining.

A train runs between Virginia City and Nevada in the summer for tourists to visit both historic towns. This area is truly filled with a good taste of Montana's unique past.

WICKES, MT., lies south of Helena on Highway 12. On September 11, 2006, we were again traveling with our Texas cousins Fred and Connie Bernhardt. We heard that there were a number of old ghost towns in this part of the state and we were out to find them. One western book stated that Wickes had quite a few coke ovens, but now there was only one left. It was used to make charcoal from coal to produce hotter temperatures for smelter work on ores.

An older gentleman was out in his yard close to the charcoal kiln. We asked him about Wickes and he said that only a few months ago, an arrastra sat near this kiln. They were on his son's land. An arrastra was used to grind down rock into smaller pieces. His son had sold the mechanism for $500 to an outsider. What a pity that we missed seeing it.

As Dave drove us up over the hill past the charcoal oven, we spotted a huge railroad trestle possibly 50 feet off the ground. The ironwork on the base of the structure was almost breathtaking. What an amazing accomplishment in the time that it had been built. We got out to take a photo and continued in our search for the huge railroad tunnel that the old fellow told us we needed to see. In about a mile, we spotted the giant tunnel ahead of us. All of us felt we had to walk inside to grasp the immense size of the opening. I guess the railcars hauled ore out of Wickes by the ton. An amazing feature of this tunnel was the set of enormous iron doors that could be closed inward. I wondered why they were needed. . .

*Bannack Days hold-up*

*Branham Lakes*

*Charter Oak Mine*

*Comet, MT mill*

*Elkhorn, MT water tower*

*Gates of the Mountains*

*Golden Sunlight Mine*

*Mammoth, Mine bank vault*

*Parrot Mine*

*Pioneer, MT dredge*

*Pony, MT school*

*Ruby, MT barn*

*Burke, ID mine building*

*Toledo Mine head frame*

# Aldridge to Storrs

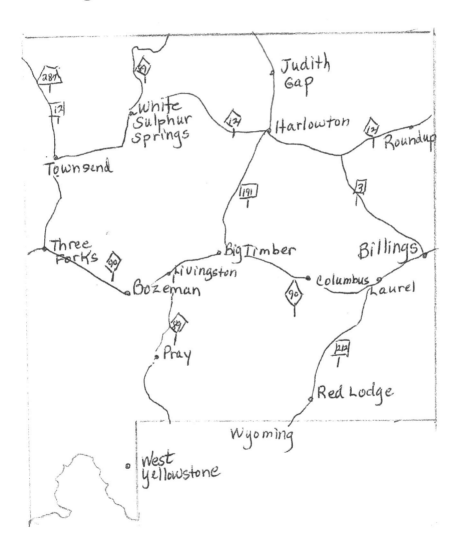

ALDRIDGE,MT, had a fascinating history. In September of 2004 we drove to Gardiner, MT, for the annual Montana Ghost Town Preservation Society conference. We had read that Aldridge lay on the "back-side" of the famous Devil's Slide, the red groove in the mountain on the way to Gardiner. Aldridge was not on our regular conference tour, so we decided to find it on our own.

We drove to Corwin Springs where the remains of a beautiful old Hot Springs resort lie in ruins with crumbling foundations. We searched out help from the nearest ranch owner to locate Aldridge. This person was Judy Jensen, a very amiable individual who helped us greatly. She lived on land that had once been part of the town Electric. (See Electric,MT) Ms. Jensen made some phone calls for us and got permission for us to drive across private land owned by the Church Universal Triumphant ranch. She also informed us that we would have to get permission in person from a Mr. Edwin Johnson to go onto the old townsite of Aldridge. She also shared that her parents had lived near the top of the hill above Aldridge and were some of the last residents living there which was quite a few years ago.

We followed Mrs. Jensen's directions up and around the hillside a few miles west of the Jensen land and saw a sign for the Johnson Guest Ranch. Fortunately, Mr. Edwin. Johnson was home that day. He said that he has a guide service with a website— montanaguide.com. He agreed to let us hike around the little cemetery and lake on his property, but he wanted us to walk with a guide, his young male employee Daniel. We agreed and soon followed the 20-something year old fellow. He went to retrieve a copy of Bill and Doris Whithorn's hardback book Photo History of Aldridge. Daniel used the book frequently on our tour, pointing out photos of buildings as they looked years ago compared to our viewing them on this day. He mentioned that there had been a tramway built from the top of the hill above Aldridge down the opposite side toward the present highway. It carried coal down to the coke ovens at Electric to make charcoal which burns hotter for smelters.

As we hiked uphill beyond the pretty little Aldridge Lake, we began seeing many old homes, wooden shanties in various stages of disrepair. For me a former teacher, the highlight of our day's hike was seeing the remains of the Aldridge schoolhouse. The bell tower was resting upright on the ground, three sides still intact, but the bell was missing. We could see the piles of lumber in the shape of the fairly large rectangular school. I was amazed to find metal frames of several old school desks lying inside the decayed walls of the fallen structure, possibly one hundred years old! Uphill to the right of the school we saw a group of small broken-down houses arranged like a tiny neighborhood on its own. Daniel told us this had been called Happy Hollow, the setting for many of the miners' homes.

Another item of real interest was a structure larger in size than most of the other houses. It was centrally located closer to the base of the town :— the first Buttreys store of Montana! Daniel told us that the first grocery shelf held 5 cans of tomatoes. Mr. Buttrey was also the postmaster for Aldridge. His store was later moved to Havre.

BELMONT, MT. lies west of Broadview off Granary Rd. This ghost town was one of the few we located that were not established because of mining. Most of the people living in this area in the past and today are farmers. We found a brochure called "Our Community" by Walter Paulson who attended Belmont High School many, many years ago. His booklet had photos of the beautiful Norwegian Lutheran Church in its prime. It had been built in 1915. In a photo of the 1990s this edifice was partially standing in a leaning position. Upon our visit in 2007, we could find only the concrete foundation and part of the front railing. Paulson's booklet stated that in the spring of 1914 most of the Belmont business district burned down. Amazingly, the next year most of the buildings were rebuilt. The crumbling base of an old school is the only remains of this public building constructed in 1917. A good-sized railroad depot sits by the tracks of the Great Northern Railroad line. It looks like a stately ghost of the past, resting in piles of dust, moved only by the wind.

BUSTEED, MT, is located about three miles north and a little bit west of Rapelje. At the present time a family by the name of Ballbach owns the property on which the ghost town rested. Mr. Ballbach was kind enough to allow us to tour the grounds of the old homestead.

The original outbuildings of the Busteed farm are in poor shape. The schoolhouse was later used as a garage, but a chimney still stands in the corner of this building. It was probably attached to a stove to heat the building when it was a school. A section of the old chalkboard remains on one wall. Nearby was the original home which had been added on several times.

The owner of the land brought out some photocopies of old news articles to share with us. Tom and Maggie Busteed were the town's namesake and started their farm and dairy about 1890. One of Mr. Ballbach's black and white photos was a picture of Mrs. Busteed holding the reins of an enormous milk cow that they had brought over from Scotland. Their home was also the post office. The old newspaper said that they were successful farmers and raised so many vegetables that they took wagon loads into nearby towns to sell. They had a huge apple orchard also. An amazing man-made earthen reservoir and diversion canal were dug out to make the water available for Busteed's gardening operation. We could see part of the mounds built all those years ago. Until we learned about this irrigation system made by Tom Busteed, I was totally puzzled about anyone in this dryland area having so much success raising huge amounts of produce!

Dave and I went to the Columbus cemetery and searched for the graves of Tom and Maggie Busteed and they were there with nice old classic headstones.

CARBONADO, MT., is found between Boyd and Joliet, MT. The only evidence of its mining past is a slag pile of coal with a large bush growing out of it. The mine was vertical about nine hundred feet. An interesting old cemetery of former Carbonado residents is seen in a fenced-in area below the nearby hill to the south.

Mrs. Betty Evertz lives nearby and "happened to be" the only house we stopped at for questions about this old mining town. She had been involved with the Joliet 4 H club that had researched the history of Carbonado and printed booklets about it and she gave us one! The brochure stated that the mine operated only four years—: 1897 to 1901. The coal from this mine supplied heat for many homes and businesses of the Joliet area in those early years.

Our first trip to **CASTLE, MT,** was in July of 2000. The day before, we had been visiting our insurance agent, Robby Robinson, and he told us about Castle because he had grown up near there. The next day, a Saturday, we headed over to White Sulphur Springs and Martinsdale to find this interesting ghost town. We were happy to find over thirty buildings spread out over the original town site. We parked and walked from one house to another, inspecting them closely and Dave started taking pictures. In the interior of one of the larger structures, we found that it still had a stairway rising to the second floor. We decided it may have been a hotel or business, not just a residence. There were several buildings with stone foundations, maybe stores or churches with owners who had spent more time and money on their construction. One tall building had the remains of a wooden trim in a curved design near the roof.

As I got close to one of the older wooden houses, a snake slithered out from under the stone foundation to greet me! I yelled and took off running as Dave checked to see what was wrong.

Recently, we learned that the farmer/rancher that owns the land on which Castle sits has restricted all sight-seers to the old ghost town. He wants people to get his permission before entering the property. I am sure that concerns of vandalism have affected this decision.

**COPPEROPOLIS, MT.,** at one time existed near White Sulphur Springs on Highway 89. Today no buildings remain on the town site. Some disturbed soil on the hills across the road indicates where the mine work had been carried out.

As we drove down a country road searching for clues to this ghost town, we noticed a nice looking Ranch-style house with a car in the driveway and we pulled into the yard. Dave went up to the door and asked the home owner who we learned was Connie Townsend if she had heard about Copperopolis. She took us into her study to get some information on the old town. As I sat waiting for her to scan an article, I looked down on the desk and spotted an invitation to John and Lavonne Deeney's 50th anniversary party in Billings. I had to say something. What a coincidence! Connie and her husband were old friends of Deeneys. I had made the cakes for their reception and we knew the Deeneys well.

Now that we had mutual friends, we visited more. A little later Mrs. Townsend offered to drive her car to the site of Copperopolis and show us in person where the ghost town had been. It was still hard to believe that there had been a thriving town there once.

One of our western history books said that Marcus Daly had bought the mining claims of this town about 1900. The article said that $250,000 in copper had been extracted from Copperopolis and that twenty-five houses and a stage station were part of the town at the peak of its mining operations. Mrs. Townsend sent some historic information on Copperopolis to me by mail. Her materials stated that the mines in this ghost town were discovered in 1866. A fact sheet that came from a man named R.M. Husbandman talked about claims being actively worked in Copperopolis in 1873. By 1899 the mine shaft went down to a depth of 1000 ft. At this time, three men's names were given with some association with the mining operation. Their names were Mr. Blewett, W.W. McDowell, and Mr. Reynolds. Another mine called the Copper Duke Mine had these names attached to it: E. M. Edwards, D. E. Folsom and N.B. Smith. Mr. John Blewett had a small hotel at that time. By 1900 these papers said that W.W. McDowell had platted a 40 acre townsite. This would be the year when Marcus Daly got involved in the Copperopolis mining operations. Our history books told us that Mr. Daly died in 1900 and these materials mention that "the estate of Marcus Daly" took up some kind of bond on N. P. This probably was the Northern Pacific claim. The mines closed in

August of 1901, but the pumps continued to work for one year or two because these fact sheets state that in February of 1903, the pumps were removed and the boilers were drained. Mrs. Townsend had one information sheet of notes from a man named Lee Rostad. The above dates on Copperopolis agreed with the Rostad facts.

COULSON, MT., was the original foundation of Billings, but it was located east of the present site. The first homes and businesses of Coulson were mostly tents and roughly-framed cabins. Some well-known Billings "founding fathers" started their first successful stores at Coulson. Alderson, McCormick, McAdow and later Yegen were some of these fine gentlemen. About 1882 the western railroad executives made the decision to move the railroad line away from Coulson and more toward the west near the Yellowstone River. Because of this, Coulson businesses relocated to the present site of Billings, establishing them along today's Montana and Minnesota Avenues in what is now our downtown area. Before long this new city began to grow as residents followed the businesses to the current location of Billings where their needs would be met. Gradually, Coulson "faded away".

The townsite of ELECTRIC is located by Corwin Springs near the Devil's Slide rock formation. Presently, it is on land owned by Mrs. Judy Jensen and also the organization called CUT (Church Universal Triumphant). We had to have permission from both owners since Electric in on private land now. Our trip there was in September of 2004.

If you look closely, you will notice a huge number of holes in brick ovens in a long row at the base of the hillside. Mrs. Jensen told us a lot about the history of Electric. She said in 1910 there were 225 of these coke ovens. They burned coal with wood chunks for 3 days with the hole sealed, then cooled it for 48 hours and it became coke. It was loaded on railroad cars and sent to Butte or Anaconda for their smelters. She pointed uphill where a tram used to carry coal from Aldridge in buckets holding 1500 lb. each. Aldridge lies on the backside of this hill. A wooden flume holding water carried coal to Electric down the same hill in other years.

The old train depot of Electric is on the ranch just east of the Jensen place. The railroad section house is 3/4th mile south. It is a gray house with two old chimneys sticking out of the roof. On the Jensen land, Mrs. Jensen showed us a big hole in the ground that was the basement of the coal company store. A small square stone building with no windows was the paymaster's office building. Further up the hill and was the old jail. It is stone and rectangular. Its doors and windows were partially restored.

A good-sized cemetery lies south of the jail at the base of the hill. We read a lot of the gravestones such as the marker for a child who died at age seven years in 1899 .I couldn't help but wonder if the death was from a childhood disease that is prevented by vaccines now. There was a mother with the last name Holbrook who lived from 1856 to 1917 and a father in a different family named Alfred Joseph Sargeant who lived from 1858 to 1901. Several graves were marked with the last name of Sommerville. As I was intently studying an old stone that was hard to read, I stepped backward and tripped over some weed-covered barbed wire. In my clumsy fall, I landed with my side and rear end on a big clump of cactus. I yelled out and Dave ran over and helped me up. I pulled up the back of my tee shirt and he started pulling out cactus spines. I'll remember that place.

Not far from Electric was a small town called CINNABAR,MT, named for the vertical dikes of red rock rich in iron in the Cinnabar Mountains nearby. (This fact came from Roberta Cheney, author of Names on the Face of Montana.) There is nothing left of this town except a few sunken stone foundations and an old bottle or can. In 1903 President Teddy Roosevelt came through Cinnabar by train to visit Yellowstone Park. He handled some national business when he stopped here so this little berg was considered America's capitol for a brief time!

We visited JARDINE, MT., in September of 2004 and 2006. In the city of Gardiner, MT., before you cross the large bridge, you will see a green sign off to the left by the Hillcrest Cabins that says Jardine is 5 miles up the hill.

In 2004 our Montana Ghost Town Preservation Society conference scheduled a trip up to this great old ghost town. The mine office was opened for us to view some historic photos of the mine operation and miners. We had a tour guide and we walked up close to the huge mill that is showing age in its wooden sections, but the old rusted metal roofs have saved some of the structure. The guide showed us the former mine superintendent's home and a few old buildings that were still standing after all these years.

In Montana Pay Dirt Muriel Wolle said that placer gold was first discovered near Jardine in the winter of 1865-66. Real production got underway thirty years later in 1899.

Harry Bush, an Englishman, was instrumental in setting up the mining operation here. He put plans in motion for a big gold stamp mill and established the town site of Jardine. Unfortunately, he overspent on this enterprise and lost his investments. After gold was mined here for several years, other ores were dug out and helped revitalize the town. Tungsten and white arsenic were two of these that were mined into the 1940s. They kept the town functioning for some time. Researchers believed that gold was the real money maker on the overall because they estimate that over 33,000 tons of gold was mined in the hills near Jardine!

At the present time there are quite a few mobile homes and rather old houses occupied by people spread out below the mill and in the hilly areas of Jardine. We saw some old miners' shacks falling apart here and there as we drove down the road exploring the vicinity.

KERWIN, WY., is about twelve miles into the beautiful wilderness area out of Meeteese, WY. There is no sign about Kerwin in the town of Meeteese so you will need to ask for directions. We found the people there were very friendly. One elderly man told us to follow him because he lived in the vicinity out of town that leads to this great ghost town. We had to drive on a rough road with two small streams of water to cross. Three Wyoming historical/government agencies combined efforts and costs to maintain about twelve original structures of the town and mill site of Kerwin. Most of the buildings have green tar paper roofs covering their tops to save the interiors of these homes, offices, and mining buildings.

Our exploration around this ghost town was very satisfying. We found several buildings that still contained mining supplies and equipment. An enormous hoist was resting in one big shack. It appeared to me like you could operate it immediately, lowering it down the deep shaft and bringing up rich soil containing gold dust or nuggets of silver. What an exciting thought! The vacant mine office looked like someone had been busy at work tabulating wages for the miners and supervisors and had just stepped outside for a smoke.

Kerwin was our turning point for carrying heavy-duty pistols to protect us against grizzly bears. On the way to Kerwin, we had seen a U. S. Forest Service sign warning that this was grizzly bear country and to be on the alert. Dave and I were both hiking around exploring buildings and just enjoying the beautiful scenery of the area. We had gone quite a distance from our pickup. Dave was around one hundred yards up a hill above me when I starting finding big clumps of bear scat (poop). Then I remembered reading that sign! I quickly put into practice some advice learned from the four books we had read about western grizzlies: "Do not startle a grizzly." I began talking loudly to Dave. As I found more piles of scat, I thought, "I don't even have a gun and Dave is carrying only a 22 caliber pistol on his waist." And my next thought,— "Where are my bells or whistles?" In no time at all, I ran up the hill and caught up with Dave. I unloaded all my fears and told him that when we get home, we are both going to buy a powerful pistol like a 357 Magnum. Actually, we did buy each of us a Taurus "Judge" because it "levels the playing field!"

LUCKY BOY MINE is found off Highway 12, east of Checkerboard, MT., on Spring Creek Road. It was remarkable to find a wooden sign indicating the distance to the old mining camp. We found a two-story house or store in fairly good shape right by the road. In the trees there were several more dilapidated houses. I yelled out when I came upon a huge hoist frame with the big fat cable still wrapped around its wheel frame. I was surprised that someone hadn't stolen some of these items for the metal content. I think I took four pictures of it!

In my research on the Internet, Lucky Boy Mine was grouped with gold mines and it showed a map. This was definitely our Montana mine, but no facts were given. We never saw the mine itself, unless, the one vertical shaft under the platform on which the big hoist sat was the only mine entrance.

As we left Lucky Boy and drove our pickup/camper down the hill, we spotted a nice public campground and decided to camp there overnight and take a walk in the beautiful wooded area.

NEIHART, MT., is a small town northeast of White Sulphur Springs on Highway 89. There appear to be miles of tailings all around both sides of the road and almost up every coulee. On our first trip to the town, we couldn't find many people around. Finally, we saw a lady in her yard. She didn't know any history, but she shared an unusual fact:— a short time before that visit, a small, narrow tornado came across a hill nearby and leveled every tree in its path for two or three miles, but never touched any houses or other buildings! We did find the place she was referring to and saw the amazing strip of missing trees. It looked like the work of an electric company that felled trees for a power line but twice as wide and there are no poles or wires.

In 2009 we stopped on Main Street at a general store with a big white sign with black lettering that read "Inconvenience Store" where two ladies gave us some helpful information about the town and said we needed to find a book on Neihart's history by a local woman named Donna Wahlberg. The book is called So Be It. A month later we bought one at the book exchange at our Montana Ghost Town conference. It was filled with excellent information and good photos.

Ms. Walberg stated in the book So Be It that the first discovery of valuable ore was in June of 1881. The lodes all ran due north and south. The rock formations were granite porphyry and quartzite. Manganese and silver were mined and then later copper and gold were discovered near Carpenter Creek. Donna Walberg wrote that by 1885 there were about 48 houses and a few businesses and by 1892 there were 135 buildings. Mining continued at a slow pace up until 1930. A train ran through Neihart until 1945. The townspeople held a huge 100 Year celebration here in 1982 with a parade, contests, booths, and stagecoach tours.

One place we were told to visit out of Neihart was the mine up Carpenter Creek. We saw a nice big mine mill up on a hill off to the left, but couldn't go there because a prominent sign said Private Road No Trespassing! We are careful to not overstep the law so we thought we might be able to get a photo from another direction. We parked our pickup. I grabbed the camera and Dave loaded his pistol on his waist. The climb up the steep hill was very difficult because there were old dry pine needles to a depth of about four inches most of the way up, so it was really hard to get a foothold most of the way. Dave was literally shoving my backside most of the way up the steep incline! That probably looked pretty funny. After we were close to the summit, I gave up. I told him it was useless because we still had to climb over the rise of the hill and I was beat. I found a nice log and sat down. He continued the hike and found the mill at a nice distance for a good photo and realized that I had the camera, not him! Well, I guess we got our exercise anyway. We both slid down the hill of pine needles to the truck, and Dave drove back out of the Carpenter Creek Canyon. He got out of the pickup and snapped a picture of the mill across the long distance where we had first spotted the old buildings..

**OHIO, KEATING, AND BLACK FRIDAY MINES** were all found south of Radersburg, MT. This location is a few miles east of Townsend. We were able to see these mines on a second time of visiting this area now in July of 2010. The first two mines are just a short distance from one another. I have to admit that I don't know which one is which because the directions given us were quite general. Of course, nothing is labeled. The more prominent mine had a huge concrete foundation covering about one-half block in length. A concrete wall about six feet high rose from the floor on the backside from the roadway. That day I found an iron ball about one inch in diameter on the ground in the interior of the concrete. It was the same kind that we handled when we toured the ball mill of Golden Sunlight. Naturally, I want to believe that this mine had a ball mill. On the floor of the concrete were dozens of wooden poles lying down parallel to one another in rows. One section's poles had been partially burned. Something else that we found here was a huge round hoist standing upright with some of the cable still attached. The hoist was about eight ft. across. Its base probably rested over the mine shaft from the looks of the frame under it. Another thing we found were tiny squares of silver—polished to a shine. Black Friday Mine was further south over a rise from Ohio and Keating Mines. Black Friday had a heavy concrete foundation which must have been the mill. Dave counted twelve different open vertical mine shafts in the area of the concrete slab. There were no warning signs for these giant holes in the earth. This is pretty scary for kids on dirt bikes or motorcycles riding around these hills. The day we visited we saw two teenage boys doing just that.

These mines were very impressive. I wondered if some of the operations here were more recent because the wooden poles were not rotten yet and the metal structures were in such good shape.

In July of 2003 we had gone to **RADERSBURG, MT.,** near Townsend to study the little town. We did photograph several old wooden structures in the area, but we never had time to locate the mines and we were losing light to take more photos anyway. Logic told us that the mine sites were probably south of Radersburg, but we wanted to drive home that same day.

Finally in July of 2010 we returned to finish our search. This was a beautiful early Sunday morning. We had spent the night before in Helena in my friend Ann Bailly's back yard in our pickup camper. We had helped her family celebrate her surprise 70th birthday.

We drove the streets of Radersburg looking for someone to give us directions to the mines. Finally, on the very last block in the west end of town, we spotted an older lady watering the plants near her greenhouse. We got out of the pickup and asked her about local history. This lady was Harla Gilespie. She gave us clear directions and specific names of three mines south of town.

Soon her husband Bill came out of the house and joined in the discussion and added some information of his own. Mrs. Gilespie stated that she worked at the Townsend museum/library regularly and she was writing a book about the history of Radersburg! We couldn't have found a more qualified person to help us! She finished by saying that in the mining years Radersburg had almost three thousand people and its citizens wanted this town to be considered in the running for state capital.

They invited us to attend their church in Townsend which was starting in an hour. We thanked them, but decided we would head south to find these local mines.

We drove several miles south and that morning we located the Ohio Mine, Black Friday Mine, and Keating Mine. That day we found concrete forms from mills, wooden head frames, a structure that we guessed may have been a small ball mill, an old rusty hoist with a cable still hanging on it, and all kinds of parts and pieces of much old mining equipment. This book will give details on these three mines under their names.

In August of 2009 we located **RED BLUFF, MT.,** which lies east of Norris, MT. Just a few years ago a huge stone hotel formerly called Scanlan's Boarding House was the main landmark for the old town, but its wooden interior burned and the heat caused the walls to crumble. Now all that is left is the stone foundation. Apparently, it was decided to clear away all the charred wood to prevent liability problems. What a terrible disappointment for us to get there too late to see that building. There were pictures of it in a couple of our western history books and it was quite spectacular.

Our history books stated that Red Bluff's mining was for gold and the town had several businesses and about 30 homes. Garnets were found in Red Bluff also by a Mr. A. W. Tanner, but the gold and silver mines brought in good revenue in the 1870s and 1880s.

Muriel Wolle stated in Montana Pay Dirt that mining was re-established in 1901 and ore yielded $14 a ton at the Grubstake Mine, good profit for that time period. A new company came to Red Bluff called Montana Revenue Gold Mining Company. They produced $3,000,000 in gold from their work here until it was shut down in 1921. A side note that Ms. Wolle offered was that two ministers, Rev. Stateler and Rev. Hargrove, came to the mining camps and held meetings for some of the three hundred workers. It was said to be well attended and the singing was enjoyed by all!

A prominent sign near the remains of the hotel states that a Research Laboratory Station is located right here at Red Bluff at the present time. The sponsor for the station was Montana State University out of Bozeman, Montana. Recently my sister-in-law Linda George shared that when my brother Gene was attending MSU-Bozeman years ago, he and Linda came out to check a seismograph in a mine tunnel entrance at Red Bluff. As part of his college job, he then recorded the readings off the machine and gave those statistics to a science lab on campus. This was in the early 1960s. (Gene spent all his working years after college as a physicist.) I didn't know any of this when Dave and I visited Red Bluff.

A short distance from RED BLUFF was a mine named BOAZ. After leaving Red Bluff, a person needs to continue on the main road about two miles. Up to your right you will see several old cement foundations resting in an upright position. This is all that remains of Boaz today. One history book said this mine only operated about ten years, but $200,000 worth of gold and silver was extracted from here. I assume that miners lived in tents or lived at Red Bluff since nothing remained of cabins.

## REEDPOINT STAGE STOP

Dave read about an old 1870 stone house used for stage coach passengers to rest located somewhere on the old Bozeman trail. He searched in a number of sources and pinned down the location to be somewhere near the town of Reedpoint, MT, but not on the present interstate highway. He drove north of town to reach the original trail and went about six miles. He spotted a lady sitting on a ditch bank close to the gravel road and noticed a man operating a large backhoe that was clearing brush out of the dry streambed.

He stopped and asked the woman if she knew anything about an old stone house. She said that she sure did and they owned it! Dave asked if he could look at it and she said to wait a short time because her husband was almost done and they would guide him up the road another mile or so to the building. The couple was Walt and Retha Scott and they guided him a couple miles farther to the stage stop house.

Dave was really impressed and took pictures of the building from different angles. They invited him to go inside and see the interior of the two story house. The structure was made of sandstone layers with mud as mortar. The interior had been updated with fixtures probably used in the 1950s. He thanked Scotts and left.

A short time later Dave brought me to Reedpoint to see this amazing building and I was equally impressed. These first trips there were in 2006, but we have been back many times to show other people and to visit the Scotts.

We suggested that they make the house into a bed and breakfast and acquire a stagecoach remodel for rides for their guests. I just knew it would work if they advertised on Internet. Walt and Retha were responsive to our suggestions, but in recent years, both of them have had health problems so these ideas were not feasible. I continue to carry a photo of the stone house in my purse because it is one of a kind. Most stage stop houses were constructed of wood and have fallen apart long ago if they were built in 1870 like this one.

As of 2011, the Scotts still own the stage stop building and property close to it, but they have leased out most of their other acreage for pasture.

**SLUICE BOX STATE PARK** was on a map shown in the Belt Creek

Canyon. It is north of Monarch, MT, off Highway 89. We immediately thought this area was a mining center because miners used sluice boxes, so we pursued the goal of finding a mine. It turned out to be a wild goose chase for mining history, but we found the beautiful Belt Creek canyon after driving downhill on a horribly rocky and curvy logging road which was a one-lane in sections.

When we reached the bottom of this logging road, there was Wolf Creek running through the canyon. We were actually on the backside of the Sluice boxes that were used for the Montana fisheries in the 1950s! A set of Lewis and Clark National Forest signboards gave all the history of this site. They said that there had been a train running through here on a trestle going to Neihart and Monarch years ago. Also silver was discovered in this area in 1879. BINGO! There was something to do with mining here.

Another sign stated that people could come on a train and receive a ten gallon milk can of trout. It was called the Fish Train. How funny!

We failed to find a mine, but we again discovered a gorgeous part of the state!

SOUTH PASS, WY., south of Lander, is very similar to Virginia City, MT., but it does not have businesses selling anything nor does it have any occupied homes. Many old, now restored, structures have been moved to South Pass and set up like a town with a main street, etc. The interiors are filled with furnishings appropriate to the pioneer days. There is a butcher shop, clothing store, mercantile store, leather goods shop, old hotel, stable for livestock, bank, etc. The tourist can look in doorways and windows to readily see what life was like for travelers long ago.

Our western history books often refer to South Pass as a stopping off place for huge numbers of cowboys, pioneers and their wagons, or gold-seekers who were coming from back east to see the West or seek a new life in Salt Lake City or on to Oregon. South Pass had a trading post for supplies and care for the travelers' animals. It must have been like an oasis in the desert!

This summer of 2012, an article appeared in the Billings Gazette about South Pass. It stated that mining and milling equipment purchased by the Wyoming state legislature and an organization called Friends of South Pass are installing these mining items into the old Carissa Mine shaft that sits right next to the ghost town.

In November of 2004, we located **STORRS** and **COKEDALE, MT.**, on the Frontage Road 89 near Livingston. For miles there is a huge number of coke ovens embedded in the ditch bank that runs parallel to the road. These stone ovens certainly speak of the past mining operations here. We noticed that these furnaces were shaped more square-like on top than the more common rounded ones we have seen elsewhere. They were large, almost the size of a Volkswagon bug. A large wooden sign gives some history of the mining work in Storrs and Cokedale years ago. The sign said that at one time five hundred people lived in this area. Its peak of inhabitants was 1902 to 1910. This sign was written and posted by the Gallatin County Historical Society and the Montana Cultural Trust. Storrs had a school, a hotel, boarding houses, a store, and a fire station.

Doris Whithorn's booklet on Cokedale and Storrs has printed photos of the coke ovens being loaded with coal off a small train and also pictures of the Cokedale plant, a big coal washer building, and a long tramway coming down the hill in 1898. I'll bet everyone in these two towns heated his home with coal. Ms. Whithorn stated that there were 130 of these coke ovens. They were built from firebrick transported from Ohio. They were loaded with ½ ton of coal. The by-product (coke) was used in smelters and was sent to East Helena, Butte, or Great Falls.

One thing that we saw that day was a humorous sight: a single, isolated round kiln had been put to use as the base of a house's foundation!

*Busteed, MT school*

*Electric, MT coke oven*

*Jardine, MT mill*

*Kerwin, WY road entrance*

*Lucky Boy Mine hoist*

*Ohio, Keating Mines author at hoist*

*Reedpoint, MT stage stop house*

*Sluice Box State Park*

# Ingomar to Ismay

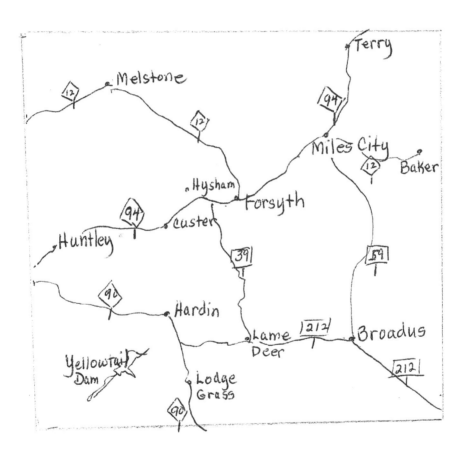

**INGOMAR, MT,** is located on Highway 12 about 25 miles east of Melstone. Very few structures remain here today. This dusty old ghost town has only a few graying buildings leaning into the wind. When the Milwaukee Railroad was completed in 1910, it brought many home-steaders from the East to settle here. The government offered them three hundred twenty acre parcels of land free and the hope for a new life. Ingomar peaked out at eight hundred residents during this time period. The town became a commercial center for sheep shearing, had a doctor, a nice school, several saloons, and established a thriving community, but ten years brought many changes. Some house fires in town, a few years of bad drought, and the Depression made hard times for the people in Ingomar. About this time also, the railroad pulled up their tracks and the townspeople moved away except for a handful of farmers and ranchers.

One business remained. The Jersey Lilly Saloon and Eatery has occupied the old First National Bank building for many years. Their famous bean soup, friendly atmosphere, and maybe its owner's per-severance have placed this business on the National Historic Register.

One summer day a few years ago, we left church in Billings to have lunch at the Melstone Bar and Café run by Dave's cousin Judy Metzger. We arrived to find a note posted on the big metal door: CLOSED GONE TO INGOMAR RODEO WITH OUR BARBEQUE. Well, there was nowhere else to eat in town and the word rodeo was like "Sic 'em" to Dave. We have gone to many rodeos in our forty two years of marriage. He watches the riders and I watch the people! So off we went with me in a dress and heels walking through dust and around manure, but talk about a good rodeo. The participants were excellent. One set of Native American cowboys in the "three man wild horse roundup" were so fast and skilled it was amazing. We had a wonderful barbequed burger and homemade potato salad at Judy's tent. It proved to be a great impression of this little town filled with dozens of pickups with gun racks in their windows and horse trailers hooked behind.

**ISMAY, MT.,** is located on Highway 12 off I 90 directly east of Miles City. It sat on the junction of the Sandstone and O'Fallon Creeks and was a popular livestock trail. For a brief time this small berg was named Joe Montana, an all-time great quarterback in the football world. A few people convinced the Ismayites to change the town's name to gain some national attention. Quite a bit of publicity followed, but it was short lived. As far as I know, the famous sports star never entered his namesake. We found one sign in town with the name Joe Montana.

Ismay was on the Yellowstone Trail route (a coast to coast road that preceded our paved roads). The Trail was in use from 1912 to 1930. Very few of these unique yellow and black Yellowstone Trail signs are still found today, but Ismay still has one posted in the center of town.

Don Baker stated in his book Ghost Towns of the Montana Prairie that Ismay was established in 1908 because the Milwaukee Railroad was built through this town just before then. Its population grew to 800.

We drove the streets of this small berg to search out other historic sites. We found an old jail, a run-down deserted hotel, and the foundation of a rather large school. We liked the historic marker in the center of Ismay that referred to a stage coach road.

# Burke to Saltese

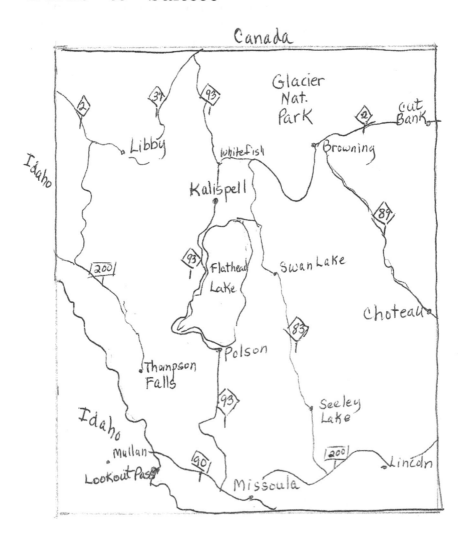

BURKE, Idaho, is a short distance north of Wallace, Idaho. In July of 2010 we drove to Lookout Pass on the Montana border to ride the fifteen mile Hiawatha bike trail for my 70th birthday. It's a breathtaking ride through 10 tunnels and over 7 trestles! Naturally, we sought out some mining towns in the area and Burke was on our destination list. The little burg of Gem, Idaho, is almost connected to Burke. As we entered Gem, we saw an elderly woman working in her flower bed. Dave stopped to inquire about any local history. The lady was very responsive to his questions. Her name was Setina Branz, a ninety-year-old widow who had lived in Gem for seventy years. Her house was once Louie's Place, a grocery store and bar, named after her late husband.

Mrs. Branz stated that the Hecla Mining Co. was forced by EPA to remove all contaminated soil from miles around Gem and Burke. She told us that last year her yard was beautiful with flowers and a vegetable garden. She said a bulldozer tore up her entire terraced flower beds, her grass, and vegetables. They replaced the dirt and grass, but only saved a few of her perennial flower plants. She was now busy planting more flowers, but much of the former beauty is gone forever. Some of her fence was removed also. She told us that Hecla Mining Co. moved to Coeur D'Alene. She thought that they sold a lot of mining stock. The CEO Sacrilege had three shifts working around the clock. She felt that they made a lot of money here. She said Hecla owns the big Good Friday mine in Mullen, Idaho, along with other properties.

As we continued north a short distance out of Gem, we saw a young man on crutches standing in his yard with a small boy. We stopped to visit him. His name was Brian Stepro. Currently he was on leave from his job at the Sunshine Mine between Wallace and Kellogg, Idaho. He had just had a motorcycle accident and injured his foot badly. He told us that he works underground taking core samples and doing engineering research to set up plans where the Sunshine Miners should do their next drilling.

Mr. Stepro mentioned that a sign nearby about the Frisco mill being blown up by a load of dynamite set off by disgruntled mine workers was a true story and well worth stopping to read. Of course, we found the sign board and photographed it.

We decided to spend more time looking over all the streets of Burke. Very few homes were occupied. The majority of the mine property consisted of piles of concrete rubble. Set back from the road were many hand-laid stone walls in various stages of disrepair. This was common on every block. Occasionally there were big piles of wooden beams, some of them oiled like railroad ties. In Burke some distance apart from each other were two sets of enormous buildings. One group was all made of red brick with big windows. This was about eight stories high. My guess is that it had been mine company of-fice buildings. The other set of buildings was made of poured concrete and connected with covered walkways. It had a tall smokestack so this must have been the mine smelter. All the structures in Burke made us think this had been a huge mining operation years ago.

COLOMA was the elusive ghost town for us. We found the old wooden buildings of the town in August of 2008 and July of 2010, but on two previous years the deep snow in the area prevented us from reaching it. It is close to Garnet out of Drummond, MT. There are only three or four miles between the two. On our first successful stop, we drove from the north close to Potomac. We had driven a few miles off Highway 200 and wondered if we would be foiled again because there was no sign of a ghost town.

Just about this time, we saw a man our age walking on the gravel road. Dave stopped and asked him about Coloma. He proved to be an ideal source of information. His name was Bob Vasecka. His father had worked at the Coloma mine for many years. He asked us to come and see his unusual "solar-operated" home. We gave him a ride the short distance and met his wife Pat also. Mr. Vasecka showed us the solar panels outside his home and the twelve huge batteries for a backup power supply in his basement. They burned wood to heat their home, but the solar energy gave them light and power for their kitchen appli-ances. Their home looked very modern and comfortable. They told us that each fall they stock up on groceries and household goods because each winter their home is snowed in. They use a snowmobile or similar motorized vehicle when they need to make a trip to the nearest town, Bonner, MT.

When we were visiting outside their home, Bob showed us a rare scene:—He was feeding Mountain Chickadees from a tiny film canister filled with chopped nuts that he held in his hand. Sometimes the birds would light on his shoulder or his head. Like a little kid, I had to ask him if I could try feeding the birds, too. Sure enough, the Chickadees flew right up to me and later to Dave to be fed. I was so glad we had our camera with us to verify this experience!

We left the friendly couple after handing them a copy of a recent watercolor I had painted of the Wells Hotel in Garnet for our Montana Ghost Town conference silent auction.

We found Coloma a little later after getting good directions from the Vaseckas. The remains of the old town were very sad. All the buildings were in terrible shape, mostly piles of lumber lying down in the shape of their original homestead. As we walked around the premises of Coloma, we found what we thought was the mill resting on the very edge of the hillside. It, too, was in ruins. We did find satisfaction in the beauty of the area and the view across the small valley below the mill. The pines here were healthy and a rich green unlike many parts of the state with the infestation of the pine needle insect disease.

In Don Miller's book Ghost Towns of Montana, he stated that pumping machines and ventilation systems had been used at this mine at Coloma. He had also seen railroad tracks leading from the mine site. This was probably in the 1970s when his book was written.

DEMERSVILLE, MT., (pronounced de.mars.vil) was the first settlement for the town of Kalispell. Its few remaining historic landmarks are found near the southern entrance to town off Highway 93. Demersville was named after one of the first business owners of town, Mr. T. J. Demers who had a mercantile store originally started as a trading post. Large black and white photos of Mr. Demers and a few of the first buildings and people in this ghost town are posted on the upper floor of the Central School Museum in Kalispell.

An article provided by a friend Sharon Loveall stated that Demersville was the head of navigation on the Flathead River back in 1886. Near the city limits of the southern entrance to Kalispell, there is still a very old rather quaint cemetery in Kalispell if you head west on Cemetery Road (how coincidental!). We read one large tombstone epitaph. This was the inscription:

In Memory of
DANIEL MACDONALD
BEN TOMKINS
JOHN CHELEY
They were cruelly murdered by Indians
In Sept. A.D. 1887 on Wolf Prairie and
Whose remains Were removed from there
And buried by order of the Coroner in this
Cemetery at Demersville
Sept. 30, 1890
*(their capitalization)*

A little bit further north and on the east side of Highway 93 is a square red building. This was the Demersville School which is now a private residence.

GARNET, MT., lies northwest of Drummond. There is a brown sign to mark the turnoff to a Frontage Road and then a short distance on that road to Garnet. Look for BEARMOUTH and BEARTOWN on your way to Garnet. Beartown had close to 5000 people in the late 1800s. Now a round saw blade nailed to a tree states: Population 2 Charlie Moore Homestead 1930.

Much of the main street of the town was burned in about 1911, but quite a few buildings remain or were rebuilt shortly after the fire. At its peak it had three livery stables, four hotels, and thirteen saloons.

During the summer months you can do a self-guided tour of this old ghost town and visit the gift shop for additional information. The old Wells Hotel that was built in 1897 is usually open for viewing and has a few antiques on display set up similar to the way it may have looked long ago. Davey's Store is close by also for viewing. We had read that in 1948 an auction was held to sell off most of its furnishings.

We had visited Garnet in 2001 and 2008 and each time we found improvements and more restoration work. On our last trip in 2010, we drove down from the north past Coloma. The most amazing thing happened! On the road close to Coloma, there was our acquaintance from two years before:—Bob Vasecka on his daily walk. He was the man that fed Mountain Chickadees from his hand and showed us his Green Energy home with solar panels and other energy-efficient features.

Before this last visit to Garnet, the U. S. Forest Service had posted several very nice sign boards of the mining history here. They were also working on a walking trail of authentic mining equipment on display outdoors. We were impressed with all these improvements.

When we were there we learned that there is an organization called the Garnet Preservation Society that raises money for this ghost town's upkeep. They were one of the groups along with the U.S. Forest Service that is responsible for some of these new additions to the grounds.

KEYSTONE MT., was rather hard to find when we tried to locate it in June of 2009. We got to Superior, Mt., and asked questions about the location. We had to go down Dry Creek Road. A very old cement railroad trestle is the clue to finding Keystone because it is like an entrance to the ghost town. Keystone had about six buildings still standing, spread over a few acres of land. One had two stories and appeared to be an old hotel or mine office. We took a few pictures of the buildings that were left. Most of them were very fragile from weather and age. Our research referred to the main mines here as excavating gold. One was called Iron King and a second one later was called Iron Queen. They apparently were combined or petered out because the last mine mentioned was called the Nancy Lee.

We were able to visit with a Mr. and Mrs. Seymour whose property had on it their modern house and a quaint little home that had been the residence of a mining family of Keystone many years ago. The Seymours unlocked the door of their rustic backyard shanty and offered to let us peer inside. It was like a step into the past, filled with their own antique collection of household items and charming decorations. They had done a fine job of restoring this treasure of the past.

These warm individuals were probably in their late fifties. That summer day a young, shy grandson was visiting them. He seemed happy to be part of the attention that his grandparents were receiving as we complimented their historical work on the old home and noticed their progress on growing a small vegetable garden in their yard also.

In July of 2010 we were in Idaho to bike the Hiawatha Trail so naturally, we needed to explore the mining history of the area near Mullen, Idaho. We learned about the LUCKY FRIDAY MINE so we inquired at the first gas station of where to go. The young man standing by the gas pump was the person we asked, and what a coincidence!:—he worked at the Lucky Friday! His name was Neal Sholey. When we asked him about tours of Lucky Friday Mine, he told us that they usually don't give tours because of the danger to the public and also there was some construction going on at the mine at the present time.

He said that they are mining lead, zinc, and silver there. Right now, the miners were at the 8,000 ft. level and planned to dig down to 10,000 ft. We learned from Neal that Hecla Mining Company now owns Lucky Friday Mine.

We drove across town to find this active mine and mill. All the buildings were painted pale green. Lucky Friday covered a large area of the town. It had a tall head frame for the deep shafts. As I viewed the number of buildings covering several blocks, I think this is a large mining operation and a good source of employment for this area of Idaho.

Brian Stepro who lives at Burke, Idaho, had told us that he thought Lucky Friday led underground to the old Burke Mine.

In June of 2009 we went to PARADISE, MT. We came into town

about 8:00 A.M. Every street was silent. We looked around for a sign of life for someone to answer questions about local history. Finally, on a side street, there sat a couple in their 40s drinking their morning coffee on their porch. She was wearing a bathrobe, but she looked up cheerfully when I stepped out of the pickup and asked, "How does it feel living in Paradise?"

They grinned and we explained that we were searching for local history. The man spoke up and said that their house had been built almost one hundred years ago, so we said it deserved a picture and Dave grabbed the camera.

They told us we should go see the old school house and cemetery that was across town. We thanked them and proceeded to find the school. It looked like it might still be operating, but this was summer and we hadn't asked the couple if it was in current use.

The cemetery had a large, old-fashioned wrought iron frame over the entrance. Some of the headstones were very old, so this graveyard must have been established in the early years of the town.

We estimated that there were only fifty to seventy-five residents in Paradise judging from the number of houses and very few businesses. The town sits in a pleasant green valley surrounded by farms and ranches in the distance every direction.

A footnote on the serious side of this chapter on Paradise:— As of April 2011, Dave died of a heart attack and went to Paradise. He could really tell us how it feels living in Paradise now, couldn't he?

PARDEE, MT., is located north of Superior, MT., but there is absolutely no sign to help you find it, so again we asked directions in Superior. We drove quite a few miles into the hills before we spotted rotten lumber in the shapes of houses. We wondered if these had been miners' shacks. We drove several miles further and thought we may have missed a turn.

Just as we rounded a corner now quite a few miles from anywhere, we came upon an old beat-up pickup with a canvas stretched over one side and propped up onto vertical boards. We realized this was a crude shelter. A primitive campfire bed was nearby and a few clothes were hanging over a large bush. We looked up to see the tenants of this backwoods home.

Three people in their twenties were standing beside the old truck:—two guys and a young woman wearing a low-cut sundress and dirty hair. I looked into the eyes of the older guy with dreadlocks and realized that he may well be "stoned" on drugs! I suddenly realized that they were living out here in the wilderness and may well be hiding out from the law!

It occurred to me that these people could easily overpower us, take our lives and then our pickup and camper and possessions and it could be weeks before we would be found. It has always been hard to report to our own children a good description of our whereabouts in all these places around the country where we go on our latest conquest to find another ghost town or mine.

As all these thoughts flooded my mind, I took Dave's hand and slowly walked forward. Dave acted very casual, too, and simply asked them if they had any idea where the remains of Pardee was. The more stable-looking young man responded that he wasn't sure what the name of the place was, but he had seen big stone foundations down the road a short distance and pointed that direction. We made a fast exit to the pickup. All I could think of was this could have been a close brush with death and now I was relieved to get away from this situation.

We drove in the direction given to us and soon found the big concrete slabs that must have been the remains of a mill from the gold and silver mining camp. We had read that Pardee's mine was called Iron Mountain. Ore was carried on wagons by mules and loaded on barges to float downstream on the Clarks Fork River to Paradise. It was then shipped out by rail to the nearest smelter. We took pictures of the hillside stone foundations and made a fast retreat to the highway!

'RIDE THE HIAWATHA BIKE TRAIL' is both an historical site and a recreational area. The location for this fifteen mile bike ride is at Lookout Pass on Montana maps. It rests on the Montana-Idaho border off Interstate 90 about one hundred miles northwest of Missoula.

The area is historic because the bike trail covers a railroad bed for the Hiawatha train about 100 years ago. It was near the western end of the route of the famous electric locomotives that the Milwaukee Railroad covered from Chicago to Tacoma. Many signboards are posted here and there along the bike trail showing photos of the construction work on the trestles and tales about the "gandy dancers"—men who labored so hard to complete this railroad base through the mountains.

The attraction for bicyclists is the beautiful scenery through this forested area. We saw hundreds of wild daisies along the dirt road that led to the parking lot of the Lookout Pass Lodge where we got our bikes to begin the day's ride. The trail is closed in the winter, but the Pass has a ski hill where skiers book their ski passes at the same lodge as bikers reserve their bikes and helmets with lights attached to go through the tunnels. There are seven trestles, some as high as 500 ft. above the canyon and also ten tunnels. The longest tunnel is 1.7 miles long. There is a fee to rent the bikes and a charge for walking or riding the Hiawatha Trail. For more information use their website: ridethehiawatha.com.

In 2010 we learned about this bike trail and I was determined to make the drive across the state to see this place. I don't like heights, especially extreme ones like some of the very high trestles. The idea of riding in dark tunnels sounded weird, but I made this my challenge. Dave had none of these fears, so when I asked him to take me there for a 15 mi. bike ride on my 70th birthday in July, he agreed. What I didn't know was that he asked our son, his wife, and our 10 year old granddaughter and 7 year old grandson to come over from Kalispell and join us. I was really surprised and delighted. The children handled the ride just fine. They each had backpacks of water bottles, sun screen, and snacks so we made occasional stops as we rode. There were latrines in a couple places along the route. I would highly recommend this special place.

SALTESE, MT., is west of St. Regis, MT. One of the first things we noticed when Dave drove into town was the very tall railroad trestle.

We didn't think that the railroad used the trestle anymore. We read that an engineer named Mr. Rogers developed an electrical system in Saltese from water power here years ago. We never heard if the system worked for long or what the outcome of his industrious invention produced.

We saw a man working on the siding of his house here in Saltese and we stopped to ask him about local history. His name was Ron Forest. He had been born in this house. He was about 55-60 years old. He had moved back to his hometown and was restoring and adding onto his parents' house. He gave us some help on finding items of interest in Saltese and the surrounding area. He pointed out the old "house of ill repute" across the street from him. I guess there were some interesting incidents that occurred there. We found this town to be somewhat like a Swiss village because it sits right at the base of tall mountains. It looked like a beautiful place in which to retire, but I'll bet the depth of the winter snow can be something to cause second thoughts on that idea.

In Memory of
DANIEL MACDONALD
BEN TOMPKINS
JOHN CHELEY
WHO WERE CRUELLY
MURDERED BY INDIANS
IN SEPT. A.D.1887.
on Wolf Prairie and
Whose remains Were
removed from there
AND BURIED BY ORDER
OF THE CORONER
IN THIS CEMETERY
at Demersville.
SEPT.30, 1890.
As a Token of respect
THIS MONUMENT is
Erected by
J. E. CLIFFORD

*Demersville, MT cemetery stone*

*Keystone, MT railroad trestle*

*Plains, MT jail*

*Ride the Hiawatha Trail tunnel*

# Havre to Zortman

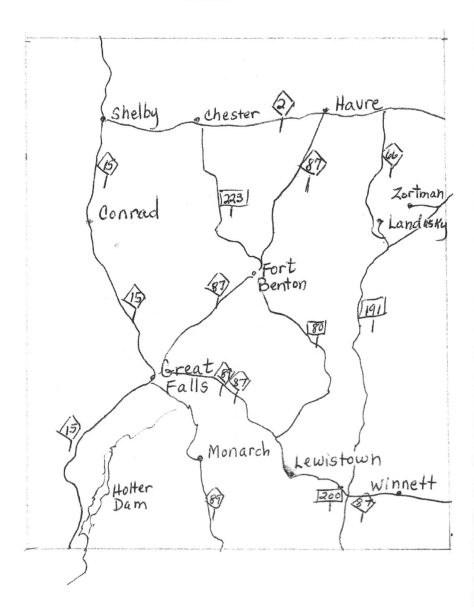

**HAVRE, MT,** is by no means a ghost town, but it certainly is full of intriguing history. The town and area around it is full of history and special sites to see. We made several trips there. Our Montana Ghost Town Preservation Society conference was held there in September of 2006. We appreciated the special speakers and guides set up for us that year.

Author Dick Wilson was our guide for more than an hour at Fort Assiniboine which had 100 buildings at one time and its own brick factory. A lot of them have been maintained for historic value. Our Bearpaw Battlefield walking tour was led by a local teacher and historian Jim Magera. He gave details of the battle and pointed out where both the Native Americans and soldiers fought for several days. He showed us where Chief Joseph surrendered and made his famous speech. Later that day we visited the Blaine County Museum at Chinook. It has an amazing panorama of the Bearpaw Battle.

On our own we went to the Havre Railroad Museum and signed up for the tour of the famous "Havre Beneath the Streets", an underground museum of real life-like displays using furniture and manikins There is a drugstore with hundreds of old bottles of medicines, a blacksmith shop, dental office, meat market ,ice cream parlor, and many more. Years ago a fire swept through Havre and burned much of the downtown. At that time a couple businesses of questionable character were operating underground. Some businessmen moved in on them and set up their own commercial enterprises. They dug out more space under the city so that they could continue to serve the public until their ground-level businesses were rebuilt. A Havre businessman decided that he would restore these shops as an underground museum. When Dave and I followed the Underground tour guide, she shut off the lights in the "basement" and we expected to be in total darkness. Instead, there was dim light coming through sections of purple glass blocks that had been set into square concrete frames about five feet across in part of the city sidewalks years ago when the businesses went underground.

We had seen buffalo jumps before but the Wahkpa Chu'gn behind the main Havre shopping mall was very professionally displayed. The buffalo bones and archeological remains are displayed under wooden house-like buildings with the earth cut away to show a cross section of the jump over a period of years. A tour guide is usually available to answer questions. We noticed one strip of the cut-away earth was blackened. Someone asked about it. The guide replied that there had been a prairie fire in the Havre area that year!

We considered **HAYS, MT.,** a ghost town, but it still has a school operating and one small grocery store called Martin's. It appeared that the large majority of its population was Native Americans. The girl that waited on us when we bought snacks at the mercantile was very pleasant and friendly.

A beautiful stone Catholic church called St.Paul's Mission Church stands out as you enter Hays. We went inside and it was very nice with a formal altar that had a full size statue of Jesus Christ with outstretched arms.

Across the street was a miniature chapel large enough for only two or three worshipers. A signboard standing nearby stated that this little church was built and dedicated by a local man devoted to his Catholic faith.

On the grass near the chapel was a bronze statue of a priest with animals around his feet and on his shoulder. The plaque on the stone base read: "In loving memory of Father Bernard Francis McMeal 1921-1994"

Our Montana map noted that a short distance out of Hays was a natural bridge. We found a sign and drove only two or three miles. What a magnificent stone formation it was. The archway was very tall with a huge opening. There were lots of trees growing near it so we got a great photo of the bridge!

On the way to locate the natural bridge, we saw a large wooden sign paying tribute to a man called Iron Man who lived from 1874 to 1959. I believe he was the keeper of the Medicine Lodge, but a section of the sign had broken off. Near the sign in a clearing were a lot of wooden poles forming some kind of Indian worship site, possibly a sweat lodge.

**KENDALL, GILTEDGE, AND MAIDEN, MT.,** are all ghost towns out of Lewistown. Our history books stated that Kendall had several stores, a bank, a Union Hall, saloons, and more. A number of these historic structures have signs with photos and facts posted in front of the buildings. I was impressed that Kendall even had a bandstand for concerts long ago. Nearby a large block of granite with deep holes in it was left from a drilling contest. The most distinctive structure here was the remains of the Union Hall. Most of the stone exterior walls still stand. It is obvious that it was a large two-story structure. I read that this union hall was not just for labor union meetings but it was also used for social events such as dances and parties.

The Boy Scouts of America have been using land here at Kendall for their summer camps. We saw signs beside the road coming into town referring to the Scouts. As Dave drove our pickup out of Kendall and around a curve, we noticed that a small mining operation appeared to be established recently. This was a weekend so no one was working and we couldn't inquire about their activities. There were several mines around here, so there probably still is "gold in them thar hills" and these men are probably drilling to see if they can find any.

GILTEDGE is about 11 miles east of Lewistown on a curving graveled road with rocky hillsides and beautiful foliage. The ghost town didn't have many buildings left. One large house was barely standing as it leaned into the wind. There were many stone foundations and small piles of gray boards that probably were miners' shacks. We read that Giltedge had a mercantile store, school, blacksmith shop, house of prostitution, and even a hospital.

After walking around the area quite a while, Dave spotted a man walking in the front yard of his farm house, the only house that looked occupied. We quickly got in the car and drove over to talk to him. What luck to find someone here. His present house was built "over" his great-grandfather's homestead. The original house was from the mining days. This man works in Billings and farms here on weekends. He told us that when WWI took place, miners were young and most of them were drafted. They packed up quickly with whatever they could carry in their wagons. Many household items were left in homes, stores, and even the hospital was deserted, leaving surgical instruments on the shelf. His grandmother stocked up on items left in the Mercantile store and the boys did "operations" on rodents in the hospital!

MAIDEN is north of Kendall. This ghost town has nothing left to show of its past history of mining. It had 1,2000 residents in its peak years, and now maybe 40 at the most. There were NO TRESPASSING signs at both entrances to the town. We drove to Maiden twice to see if we could get photos or visit a resident and found no one. It is hard to believe that $3,000,000 worth of gold came out of this area. We found one historic sign about Maiden near the town.

LANDUSKY,MT, lies directly north of Billings. You need to drive to Grass Range on Highway 19 and watch for signs, but it is about 4 hours from Billings. When you enter town, off to the left you will see the old Landusky cemetery with its tall weeds and wooden grave markers. The namesake of the town, Pike Landusky is buried there. It is worthwhile to research biographical sketches of him. He was a sharpshooter and a tough character who came west alone at a young age and made a name for himself. He was killed by the well-known outlaw Kid Curry, a traveling companion of Butch Cassidy and the Sundance Kid.

As we drove the road into this small ghost town, we saw several men working on playground equipment in front of an old white schoolhouse. This was 2002 and the school had eleven students. At this time it was holding a record of Montana's longest continuously-operating school. We learned later that it had closed due to the low school population. We asked the guys in the front yard if any of them knew any history of Landusky. One man grinned and said that there was an old guy inside who knew a lot about it. He was the grandpa in the family and these were his relatives.

We walked inside and shouted "Hello". There was Winston

94

Mitchell. He was very responsive to our questions and proved to be very amiable and helpful. He told us where to see the Pike Landusky homestead. Mr. Mitchell pointed up the mountain to where all the gold was mined. He said the road to the mine was closed to the public. He stood under two framed pictures: —Washington and Lincoln in the old-fashioned classroom with a green chalkboard like the one I used when I started teaching in 1962. Mr. Mitchell gave us a short tour of the building. The current teacher was in another room preparing for the school year. There were four computers in the adjacent room. What a contrast from our first impression of the old building.

This elderly gentleman bragged about the Phillips County Museum in Malta and encouraged us to go there. He had invested time and money working there. He was a good promoter for it because we did end up staying over an extra day to drive there.

We decided to go down the road to see the Landusky house now with a modern red metal roof. The structure looked pretty good now, but it was the original home of town's namesake. He had married a widow lady and helped raise her big family in that home. There were just a few buildings in the town. We could not see many signs of the big gold mine, just the disturbed soil up on the hillside. We had read about extensive reclamation work up on the mountain.

In 2011 our friends Bill and Gisela Maehl invited me to ride along to Landusky and Zortman. He was the mining engineer in charge of the reclamation these past years and he needed to check the amount of damage done to the hills and new plant growth from the 2011 spring floods. He estimated a possible $2,000,000 flood damage on the day that I rode with them to these two ghost towns. On this recent trip, I got to see the actual gold mine sites because of Bill's authority to drive on roads restricted to the public.

ZORTMAN, MT., is directly north of Billings, but it is over 4 hours away. You drive to Grass Range on to Landusky first and watch for signs to Zortman. This area was rich in gold ore, and also rich in history. For instance, Butch Cassidy and the Sundance Kid were supposed to have a hideout in this part of the state. Also tales of the notorious Loman brothers (Kid Curry was one of them.) abound here also.

In August of 2002 we found that Zortman sat at the base of tall hills one way and a plain in the opposite direction. On a little mound of a hill sat a small but beautiful white church with a pointed steeple. A few businesses still exist in the "almost ghost town". We saw a humorous sign:—Zortman Motel and Garage. We stopped to ask about local history and found the young couple, John and Candy Kalal, who owned this enterprise, were very outgoing and helpful. We wanted to see the mining area and mentioned that to John Kalal. He spoke up, "You'll never make it up there in that outfit!" He was referring to our small pickup with a shell on the back which was not a 4 wheel drive. He added, "I'll take you up there in mine if you can wait a little bit. He loaded his two little daughters in his truck with us and off we went on a very rocky, rough road through thick brush and trees. He drove through streams of water twice and pointed out interesting sights all along the way. We were gone for over one and one-half hours and when we returned, he would not accept any money for his gas or his time.

Later that afternoon we hiked around the streets of Zortman and found a café for supper. At the far end of town we noticed an interesting road and we walked through an open gate and discovered what must have been a cyanide pond used to separate gold from other material. It smelled awful and was lined with black plastic. We realized that maybe we weren't supposed to be here! Oh, well, it was our first sight of one of these chemical treatment ponds. We had read about them and now got to view one.

We booked a room at the Zortman Motel and Garage. and noticed people outside the motel looked like they were panning gold from a huge gravel pile. I looked up and recognized the lady who had a gold pan in her hand. It was Peggy Arnott, an acquaintance from Billings. I asked if she was finding any gold and she showed me a little gold dust in her hand. Wow!

When we visited with Kalals the next day, they said that quite a few of the people who came to Zortman were archeologists who were there studying the rock formations in the area. There is a huge cave in the mountain not far from town. They said that at the present time it is closed to the public. John said, "You know the streets here are paved with gold!"

Now after Dave died in April of 2011, a month later, I was invited to ride along with our friends Bill and Gisela Maehl to see the mine reclamation up on the mountains of Zortman in areas that the public could never visit. Bill has been the mining engineer in charge of the reclamation work of both Zortman and Landusky. This was an eleven hour day from Billings and back. Bill also showed me photos of the mountain from an airplane view. I felt very grateful to go to the top of the mountains where the gold mining took place.

*Hays, MT natural bridge*

# Enchanted Highway to Medora Musical

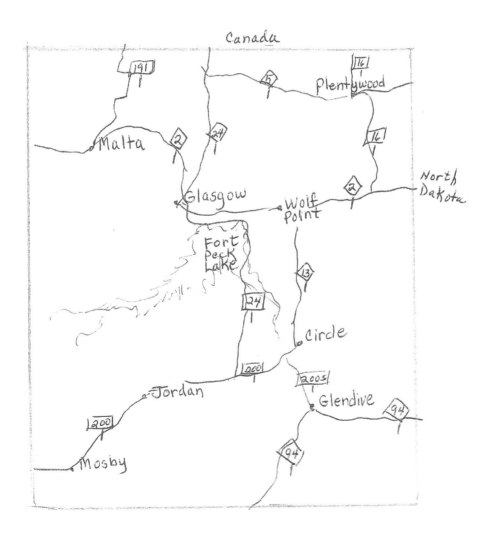

## ENCHANTED HIGHWAY

Most North Dakota maps now label the 50 mile road from Gladstone to Regent the Enchanted Highway for its amazing metal sculptures all designed and welded by one man who grew up in Regent:— Gary Greff.

There are about 10 different and unique metal sculptures. They are spaced a few miles apart on this special highway. Can you imagine a 50 ft. high grasshopper, a 70 ft. long pheasant, or a tin family each about 44 ft. high? One art form is called Geese in Flight. It was raised up and put in place in 2001. The next year the Guinness Book of World Records rated it as the largest scrap metal sculpture in the world. It weighs over 75 tons! The largest goose in this grouping has a 30ft. wing span

The day that we drove over the Enchanted Highway and photographed each set of sculptures and finished on the south at Regent, North Dakota, we stopped to visit the little store that sells souvenirs about the art pieces along with an ice cream parlor. We were introduced to the artist/welder Gary Greff. We asked him to autograph our postcards and Dave asked him to pose for a photo with me. He was very cordial and friendly. He told us about his plans to make more metal sculptures in the future.

It is well worth the drive on I 94 to Dickinson, North Dakota, area to view these huge art pieces.

## MEDORA MUSICAL, North Dakota

If you haven't heard of Medora's summer spectacular night show, you will want to make a visit there. The performances are held in an outdoor amphitheater looking down on a colorful stage of life-size buildings that can be moved into different settings. Young energetic singers/actors present a lively show in mostly western costumes. The summer brings a change of show every few weeks, so local people can see a variety of performances throughout the season.

We enjoyed the somewhat patriotic theme and the professional quality of the singers and dancers with some comedy added. The show finished in the dark with fireworks so beautiful in the open air arena with a perfect view of the action and colors.

Next door prior to the performances, a pitchfork steak fondue is offered also. I am sure that tickets can be purchased ahead of time on Internet.

The city of Medora has several other historic sites to visit. The Chateau de Mores State Historic Site is an estate with a mansion overlooking the city. The Marquis's wife was named Medora von Hoffman, the town's namesake.

The Theodore Roosevelt National Park is only 5 ½ miles away. It is a drive-through road with hiking trails. We saw a herd of bison right beside the roadway when we drove there.

In Medora we attended a play called "Bully". One actor presented a dramatic autobiography of Teddy Roosevelt. He did an excellent job. The next morning when we went out to breakfast at a local restaurant, we noticed this actor. Dave went over and complimented him on the fine job of acting he had done in this play. He was very cordial and allowed Dave to take a picture of this man and me.

Medora has motels, an R V park, a few restaurants, tourist and coffee shops. Visitors are warmly greeted in this little town.

*Enchanted Highway, N. D.fishing sculpture*

# FORTS OF THE 1800s

## WESTERN MONTANA

In the Missoula area there are three forts: Fort Owen, south at Stevensville, Fort Missoula right in the city, and Fort Fizzle on Highway 12 west of the city. FORT OWEN was started in 1841 by Father Pierre Jean DeSmet. This priest came to the Bitterroot Valley to set up a church called St. Mary's Mission. Father DeSmet provided help to the local Native Americans for nine years. When struggles arose, John Owen took over and made this a trading post. He married a Shoshoni woman named Nancy. and was appointed an agent for the Flathead Agency. For a number of years they successfully raised crops and even had a flour mill. In 1872 Mr. Washington McCormick purchased Fort Owen. When he died, his family kept the name of the post as Fort Owen and donated an acre of land and the remains of the fort to the state of Montana. This is what is left today: an elongated stone structure divided into several rooms. It has beautiful old rustic wooden doors. On site there is the foundation of the grinding mill and a root cellar. A sign is posted nearby with some worthwhile facts about this fort. Fort Owen is on the National Register of Historic Places. FORT MISSOULA was built in an open wilderness area but now it is surrounded by homes in the western end of Missoula. Michael Koury's book Military Posts of Montana stated that Generals Sherman and Gibbon were involved in establishing this fort. It was well built with beautiful two-story officers' quarters in the 1890s, but its use diminished and by 1915, not much was left of the structures. Today we found one major brick building with an excellent museum and bookstore. The grounds are occupied with a forest service lookout tower, an antique "working sawmill", the old Grant Creek School, and an amazing building: a World War II Internment Camp dormitory! Photos and captions on the interior walls told us that it housed three nationalities: Japanese, German, and Italian prisoners. I was glad to hear that some of these people were allowed to work in stores and businesses in Missoula. FORT FIZZLE is found 10 mi. west of Lolo, MT. There is a sign to lead you to the location. There are no buildings here and never were. Late in June, 1877, Cavalry soldiers were on the trail of Chief Joseph and his followers. Military men prepared a mound of felled logs in a type of makeshift fort to prepare for a possible confrontation. As the soldiers were madly chopping logs and piling them up for protection, Chief Joseph quietly led his people across the hill above the siegeworks and passed out of sight—-thus the plan fizzled! Isn't that funny? South of Flathead Lake on Highway 93 near Pablo, MT, is FORT CONNAH. One single old cabin sits in a pasture off the east side of the road, one of the oldest buildings in Montana. This fort was a trading post for Native Americans and fur traders back in 1847. A man named Angus McDonald ran the business. There were originally two structures here and someone in our Montana Ghost Town Preservation group heard that plans are underway to do more restoration work and build another house.

## CENTRAL MONTANA

In the Livington-Bozeman,MT, two forts were built: Fort Ellis and Fort Parker. FORT ELLIS was east of Bozeman. An agricultural experimental station of MSU-Bozeman now sits on the premises of the old fort. None of the buildings exist anymore. When we found the location, some college students were working in the yard. None of them had even heard that a large fort with 40-50 buildings had been there! Later we learned that a good display case of artifacts picked up from the earth around the fort plus other historic photos were available to view at the Pioneer Museum in Bozeman. There is little reason to visit Fort Ellis today since nothing remains. FORT PARKER was established nine miles east of Livingston, MT. There is a brown sign on the Interstate to show where to take the the Frontage Road. Up the small hill a semi-circle of large colored signboards tell the history of Fort Parker. The first Crow Agency of Montana was here. We contacted the owner of the Mission Ranch adjacent to the site of the fort. He is Doug Ensign and he loaned us a folder of letters, documents, and materials on the fort's history. He referred us to the Yellowstone Gateway Museum in Livingston, MT, for an excellent coverage of Fort Parker's history. It was started as a farming enterprise for the Crow Indians, but frost, floods, and grasshoppers caused crop failures. The first wooden buildings went up in fire in 1872. A few adobe brick structures replaced the burned houses. By 1874 the Crow Agency moved to Absarokee, MT. Only a few rough foundations remain today.

Northwest of White Sulphur Springs, MT, FORT LOGAN was built. It originally had about twenty houses, a large horse stable and a blockhouse. The beautiful blockhouse has been preserved and most of the long horse barn remains. A large informative sign is posted nearby. The peak of operation was 1875 according to Michael Koury who wrote .Military Posts of Montana. There were 95 enlisted men here. The fort closed in 1880.

FORT ASSINIBOINE is located seven miles southwest of Havre, MT. It was one of the largest western military forts. There were over one hundred buildings constructed. There are about twenty structures left today. We were very impressed. At a Montana Ghost Town Society conference, we walked the grounds and had author Dick Wilson guide us. Because the fort had its own brick factory, many of those buildings were made of brick and survived these many years. We were told that Lt. John Pershing was the commander here and the Tenth Cavalry of Negro soldiers was stationed at Fort Assiniboine. The government abandoned the fort in 1911.

Two Montana forts were in the Great Falls, MT, area. FORT BENTON is northeast of the city and FORT SHAW was built west of Great Falls on Highway 21. Fort Benton fort rests inside the city of Fort Benton, MT. We liked our visit to Fort Benton. The people were friendly and informative. Three museums are in the community. On the boulevard of grass along the Missouri River there are many large historic signs and bronze statues of Lewis, Clark, Sacajewea, and the dog Shep that had waited at the train station six years thinking his deceased master would return. A large replica of the keelboat Mandan is displayed there, too. One of the fort's blockhouses has been restored perfectly and next door is a replica of a trading post. Inside were Hudson's Bay blankets, plugs of tobacco, etc. and a gentleman dressed as a proprietor of the business like it was years ago. He told us that if the community can raise the money, Fort Benton will build three more blockhouses as close to the original design of the fort as possible. While we were sightseeing in the town, we saw the Grand Union Hotel, totally restored like years ago as a hotel and restaurant. The old bridge over the Missouri River can no longer hold the weight of vehicles, but it is used as a foot bridge and historic site for photos. FORT SHAW is close to the town of Simms on Highway 21. There are several old buildings left from the fort, but no informational signs or a museum. We read in <u>Military Posts of Montana</u> that this fort was not used very long—:established in 1867 and closed down in 1891. It was a Regimental Headquarters. The post kept one year's supply of provisions on hand. Apparently in the 1970s the Fort Shaw buildings were occupied by a government agency, but our research was skimpy. In 1904 a basketball team of Native American girls who lived at this fort made <u>national</u> news. They played dozens of other teams and always won. They made it to the World's Championship at the St. Louis World's Fair and won first place! Books have photos of the girls posed in leather dresses, beautiful moccasins, and long braided hair when they traveled.

FORT YELLOWSTONE was the original name for Mammoth Hot Springs in Yellowstone National Park because this location was first a military fort before it was made a national park in 1872. All the old beautiful brick buildings with the tall chimneys were military officers' quarters and the large buildings made from natural stone had other uses by the Cavalry such as a mess hall or barracks.

## EASTERN MONTANA

Two old forts are only about 20 miles from Sidney, MT. They are Fort Buford and Fort Union. FORT BUFORD did not have much to see of its historic past. There were just a few restored buildings when we went there in 2003, but there was construction going on for another soldiers' barracks or officers' quarters. One significant fact about this fort is that it was here that Chief Sitting Bull surrendered to the military. FORT UNION was very impressive. It has been totally replicated like it was built in 1828. There are four blockhouses on the corners covered in white stucco like the old adobe. The walls are several feet thick of huge poles. Inside the walls, the earthen floor has outlines of other buildings that were in existence long ago. Inside the fort and straight ahead is a huge white two-story building that had been Officers' Quarters. It is now a very nice museum with rooms for staff or care-takers of Fort Union. When we were visiting in the summer, several people were dressed in costumes walking around. This fort was chiefly a trading post so one man in buckskins was selling twists of tobacco and colored beads (probably made in China). John Jacob Astor of the American Fur Company was in charge of this fort in its first years. At its peak, almost one hundred people kept it going. It operated until 1867. I recommend a trip to northeastern Montana to see Fort Union, prefer-ably in the summer.

FORT CUSTER was located about 30 miles east of Billings, MT. It is south of the Big Horn River. Nothing is left of the fort today; however, there is a sturdy concrete obelisk by the Frontage Road. It states a brief history of Fort Custer on it. We read that after General Custer and his Cavalry were defeated in 1876, this fort was quickly constructed the next year. The buildings were made on a high bluff above this Big Horn valley. Nine companies of men were assigned here eventually, but it was abandoned in 1898.

FORT KEOGH is found on the west end of the town of Miles City, MT. It was on the junction of the Yellowstone and Tongue Rivers. Michael Koury's book Military Posts of Montana states that thirty buildings were constructed here in 1877 until a total of sixty made up the total housing and storage structures. At Fort Keogh's highest point of importance to the military, there were 36 officers and 754 enlisted men stationed here. In the early 1900s the need for protection for citizens had lessened and the fort closed. Today a livestock experiment station uses some of the remaining buildings, but a few historic structures are on site: a brick water wagon house with a metal plaque mounted on it, one restored officers' quarters, and a large white wooden two-story barracks. Across town in Miles City is the impressive Range Riders Museum that is housed in five different buildings! One of these was from the fort. Some of Fort Keogh's history is displayed at this museum.

## NORTH DAKOTA FORTS

FORT ABRAHAM LINCOLN is a state park south of Mandan, N.D. covering a couple acres. Several buildings have been restored : a large soldiers' barracks, some blockhouses, a cavalry post, and a commissary made into a bookstore now. Before Custer's defeat in 1876, the general and his wife lived here. Their beautiful residence burned with only a few personal items saved. The state of North Dakota used a photo and built a close replica of their home here at Fort Abraham Lincoln. We paid to take a tour with a young man dressed in an authentic-looking Cavalry uniform. We found it very worthwhile to see this fort. FORT CLARK was built between Washburn and Stanton, N.D. on Highway 200. When we located the site of the fort, we were very disappointed to find almost nothing—no buildings and only one small historic sign about the fort that had been established in 1831 by James Kipp of the American Fur Company. FORT MANDAN is located on Highway 83 South between Minot and Bismark, N.D. This fort has been re-constructed here as a full-size fortress with wooden poles standing upright for walls. It covers about ½ city block in size. Visitors can walk around the grounds and view the interior of the fort just like you were one of Lewis and Clark's men who wintered at Fort Mandan in 1804-05. The North Dakota state historians have filled the interior with fire pits, wooden benches, furs hanging, moccasins being sewed, and animal skin clothing lying about. You almost feel like you are intruding in someone's home! You will enjoy your visit here.

## FORTS OF WYOMING

FORT BRIDGER is in southwestern Wyoming off Interstate 80. We drove to this fort in September of 2005 not realizing this was the weekend of the annual Mountain Man Rendezvous. It was almost impossible to find the old historic fort buildings among the hundreds of people, numerous tents, and vendors' tables. It proved to be fun once we relaxed and got into the spirit of the celebration instead of concentrating so hard on exploring the fort. Many people were dressed as pioneers, traders or trappers in buckskins and high boots or moccasins, and dance hall girls, etc. Quite a few Native Americans were in full regalia costumes, performing dances on a stage periodically throughout the day. I swore I saw Abraham Lincoln walk past me!

We located the actual restored buildings of Fort Bridger and the impressive replica of the trading post started by Jim Bridger and his business partner Louis Vasquez in 1843. This was an elongated log cabin with a sod roof. Historians had placed hides, furs, blankets, and foods like jerky inside. The old trading post was successful also because of the fertile Green River valley.

FORT BROWN was the original name for Lander, WY. No semblance of a fort remains today and only one small sign on a business at 5th and Main mentions the fort. A magnificent metal sculpture of a bison stands in front of this building. The artist was Lyndon Pomeroy.

FORT CASPAR is three miles west of the city Casper, WY. Note the two spellings. A brochure said this fort was first called Platte River Bridge Station, but changed to honor Lt. Caspar Collins who was killed in a battle near Casper. Our research found that a ferry was built here in 1847 and later the Pony Express set up a relay station at the site of this fort. About 1866 the Union Pacific Railroad laid tracks across this area and the need for a military establishment diminished. Troops were ordered to Fort Fetterman and some of Fort Caspar's buildings were sold or moved off site. In 1933 historians used sketches of the original fort and constructed the first building like the old one. Unfortunately, that structure burned down during a re-enactment scene using flaming arrows! Three years later, the WPA program provided some funds and workmen to construct several replicas of the original fort. By 1983 local civic leaders had continued on this task until today there are several nice fort buildings, a replica of a section of the old bridge and a very nice museum. We enjoyed our visit there very much.

FORT FETTERMAN is found south of Sheridan, WY, near Douglas. Its use was short-lived. It was built in 1867 by four companies of infantry soldiers, but closed in 1882. Our history books said that General George Crook stationed his men here off and on as he went into Indian battles across Montana and Wyoming. Many Native Americans fled to Canada and the conflicts lessened. The state of Wyoming took over acreage and the remaining fort buildings in 1967 and restored some of them. An Officers' Quarters became a museum later. A tall stone monument stands as a memorial to the 81 military men including Captain William Fetterman who were killed by Crazy Horse and about 2000 warriors in December of 1866. The cavalry had left the fort to rescue a wagon train and were ambushed over a hill some distance away.

FORT FRED STEELE is found directly east of Rawlins, WY. We drove some distance to locate it, but there really is nothing here but foundations of buildings and two tall chimneys standing bleak against the sky and one small ammunition storage house made of rough stone. In our research later we learned that Fort Steele was not primarily a military post, but was loosely established with 300 men living in tents. Basically, they were taking turns protecting railroad workers laying tracks for the Union Pacific Railroad from Omaha, Nebraska into Utah. Later the military encampment became a small fort of both wood and stone structures. After the trains were operating, some civilians lived on this post working as blacksmiths and wheelwrights, but by 1886, Fort Fred Steele closed.

FORT LARAMIE is three miles south of the town of Fort Laramie, WY, on Highway 160. According to a brochure on this historic site, it was one of the largest western forts. Its location made it a good trading post for frontiersmen, pioneers moving west, and later for Native Americans to trade furs for their necessities. By 1890 Fort Laramie had 60 buildings. Even though many of the adobe buildings are just large white skeletons now, there are many other nicely restored barracks, Officers' Quarters, an old Guard House where delinquent soldiers were imprisoned, a bakery, a huge mess hall, and an impressive Visitors Center/Bookstore. Overall, this fort covers acres. It took us almost two hours walking in and out of these nicely restored buildings. We visited in the summer and enjoyed seeing men dressed in authentic looking Cavalry uniforms in several buildings available to answer questions or point out highlights of the post that might be missed.

FORT MCKINNEY is located south of Buffalo, WY. Today the land that was once occupied by this fort is now covered with buildings of a Veterans' Home. The only structure left from the fort today is a two-story white wooden hospital. Inside was a miniature model of Fort McKinney and a display case with some interesting artifacts recovered from the fort. There weren't any brochures of information to enlighten us on its history.

FORT PHIL KEARNY is found on I 90 between Sheridan and Buffalo, WY. We had learned that this fort was designed like a true stockade with 8 foot walls enclosing about 15 acres of land. One leaflet said that 4000 logs and 130,000 bricks were used in the construction back in 1866. What a disappointment to find only signs marking flat stone foundations of about 40 old military structures and one good-sized Museum/Bookstore. We learned that a government treaty with some Native American tribes in 1868 agreed to close down forts on the Bozeman Trail so this well-built fort was abandoned by the Army and soon afterward, Cheyenne Indians burned it to the ground. Obviously, it was never restored. The Museum did have a diorama of two battles fought close to this area: the Fetterman Battle and the Wagon Box Fight.

FORT WASHAKIE is 15 miles north of Lander, WY, on Highway 287. No buildings from the fort remain today, but many good informational sign boards are posted here. Nearby is the beautiful Sacajewea

Cemetery. It covers about two city blocks. Most of the graves were decorated with flowers or memorials. A full-sized bronze statue of the famous Indian lady was erected here. Her stone monument is placed in the center of her two sons' graves: Jean Baptiste Charboneau (who was with the Lewis and Clark Expedition) and Bazil , her nephew that she adopted. We investigated information on Chief Washakie, for whom the fort was named and learned that his mother was a Lemhi Shoshone and his father was a Flathead Indian. He was known as a wise leader and a peacemaker. He helped acquire land for the Wind River Reservation and he promoted free access to the mineral water at Thermopolis, WY, for all people. Sounds like a great man!

*Fort Assiniboine headquarters*

*Fort Benton, MT hotel*

*Fort Bridger, WY Officers quarters*

*Fort Yellowstone (Mammoth)*

CPSIA information can be obtained at www.ICGtesting.com
Printed in the USA
LVOW02s0712060514

384596LV00005B/16/P